Time to Go

Time to Go

Alternative Funerals

The Importance of Saying Goodbye

Jean Francis

iUniverse, Inc.
New York Lincoln Shanghai

Time to Go
Alternative Funerals

All Rights Reserved © 2004 by Jean Francis

iUniverse, Inc.

For information address:
iUniverse, Inc.
2021 Pine Lake Road, Suite 100
Lincoln, NE 68512
www.iuniverse.com

ISBN: 0-595-31859-2

Printed in the United States of America

To my Dad whose God was everything natural, kind and loving.

Tommy Morgan
(1907–1985)

CONTENTS

FOREWORD

This book by Jean Francis is a very good contribution bringing home the idea that funerals can be celebratory, unique and very personal. The most environmentally friendly funerals are green burials, which take place on private land or in woodland burial grounds, which are now increasingly popular and springing up all over the country.

Thanks to the tradition of the Quakers who often buried their dead in their gardens or orchards, in Britain there exists no law which demands that a person must be buried in consecrated land.

In 1991, when Nicholas Albery and I started the Natural Death Centre, we knew very little about the world of palliative care, the funeral business or bereavement. We set up the centre because we felt there was a need for death education, a place where ordinary people could come to learn about death, embracing it as a natural part of life—learning about what was needed in order to support someone who wished to die at home.

We were inspired by the Tibetan Buddhist view, which contemplates death as a way to live as fully as possible in moment-to-moment awareness, knowing that our physical life is impermanent. Funerals were not on our minds at that time. But we rapidly became experts on green funerals with help from John Bradfield who had researched the law surrounding burials. We were also encouraged by the demand of the public, who wanted funerals such as Jean writes about in this book. The Natural Death Centre, London, now advises on the law and practice surrounding private land burial and has founded the Association of Natural Burial Grounds.

Since the first green burial ground was set up, by Ken West in 1993 as part of the cemetery in Carlisle, there are now over 180 green burial grounds in Britain and the number is still growing.

Planning your own funeral and discussing the plans with your loved ones when you are healthy and well is a useful and very therapeutic thing to do. The Natural Death Centre runs many workshops on this topic. Tragically, it has been very useful to us, when close friends have died, being able to help organise green funerals for them.

In 2001, Nicholas was killed in a car crash aged 52. Knowing what his funeral wishes were and carrying them out for him was a hugely healing experience for our family and friends. Everyone was inspired by what turned out to be a spiritually uplifting occasion.

I think of a funeral as a ritual that marks the end of a life, and the start of a new life, which we have not yet begun. I believe the mourning period is a time of 'becoming'—a period of limbo between the old and the new. The funeral is an opportunity of coming together, to bring the person who has died alive to us, to have a sense of them in their totality—through the telling of memories that reflect on the many aspects of the person who has died, allowing us to reflect on feelings which, like a symphony, swell and recede. In this way a funeral can provide a space for healing and begin the process of integration and meaning, finding a place for the person who has died, who continues to be part of our lives and of our story. Sadness, joy and gratitude can become interwoven, as are life and death.

Planning ahead of time is good, because it allows us to be prepared, not just for the funeral and bereavement, but also for living and ageing. In the words of Elizabeth Kubler-Ross:

> *If you can face and understand your ultimate death, perhaps you can learn to face and deal productively with each change that presents itself in your life.*

Wishing you a long and happy life!

Josefine Speyer
April 2004

AUTHOR'S NOTE

I grew up with an all-consuming fear of death, that someone close to me, or my pet, would die. As a child I cried relentlessly over a picture book in which a kitten had fallen into a pail of milk because I feared it would drown. To console me, another picture was stuck over the offending scene. Even more ridiculous was my horror at the burning of dead flowers on a bonfire!

By contrast, when my young brother's goldfish died he buried it in a tobacco tin with great ceremony. Morbid curiosity led him to examine it regularly and everyone was encouraged to take part. As a family we have always had pets, and following the death of each one the heartache was always unbearable. We pay the price of love!

Traditionally, families gather together to celebrate the three main milestones of life—birth, marriage and death. During my thirty-six years in the party planning and catering business, clients chose to celebrate these occasions in many different ways. Following a burial or cremation, a reception usually takes place where families and friends can gather together. It could be in a private house, hall, garden, woodland, or sometimes, as in my case, in a delightful room within the funeral director's premises.

For unloading, the catering van had to be parked alongside the fleet of hearse which meant everything had to be carried past the coffins awaiting departure with their gleaming brass handles and name plates. Initially I felt extremely squeamish at this close contact with the dead but eventually my curiosity led me to ask to be taken on a guided tour of the premises. My uneasy feelings eventually developed into a macabre fascination. The loss of my Dad forced me to look death right in the face.

Visiting bereaved families to discuss their catering requirements gave me the opportunity to do a lot of listening. I was also able to offer suggestions that would soften the edges of a sad occasion, such as to display photographs of the deceased and memorabilia. Often this would stimulate conversation and even evoke laughter. We provided welcome cups of tea, homemade cakes and savouries including all the family favourites.

A longstanding client requested in her will that we cater for her funeral reception. She had never been a person to argue with, so we carried out her wishes to the letter, fearing she might come back to haunt us! I believe in a life after death, but some of my catering helpers were somewhat sceptical. Nevertheless, we all experienced many strange phenomena whilst catering for funeral parties. Here are a few examples:

- A violent thunderstorm accompanied an elderly gentleman's funeral, which was at 3pm. His widow recalled their wedding day fifty-three years earlier, when at exactly the same time of day a thunderstorm had interrupted their vows.
- Electricity supplies have been cut off and telephone lines gone dead on many occasions while the neighbours' have remained unaffected.
- Following a memorial service in a church hall, the deceased's daughter was thanking us for 'a job well done'; she also mentioned the beautiful service conducted by the Minister. At the mention of his name one of the many damp tea towels rose into the air, swirled around the kitchen and landed at her feet. It was one with a print of the church in which he ministered.

There have also been some embarrassing memories:

- Having set up a sumptuous afternoon tea beneath a veranda, dripping with roses, we waited. There was not a mourner in sight; having double-checked, we realised we were a week too early!
- Two halls with similar names led us to deliver a funeral feast to the wrong location; never was there such a rapid transfer and such red faces!

People's reaction to death varies considerably. There are those who happily imagine themselves sitting on a fluffy cloud strumming a harp, whereas others dismiss their mortality with comments like 'flush me down the loo' or 'a black bin liner will be fine!'

The Mexicans, like some other cultures, celebrate death with a festival—'The Day of the Dead' where souls return briefly to rejoin their loved ones. Offerings of food and drink are set out in graveyards with candles, flowers, fireworks, and skulls and skeletons mimic the living while a party mood prevails. The celebration takes place annually for several days from 31st October.

The Natural Death Centre in London organises a national 'Day of the Dead' annually on one Sunday in April, which is a peculiarly British affair.

Graveyard walks are now a popular tourist attraction. Cemeteries are seen as places of historical and environmental interest, to be visited by the public with guided tours available.

While collecting information for this book I interviewed people from many different walks of life, ages, faiths and beliefs. A few have asked, "Whatever is there to write about funerals other than burial or cremation?"

Many people have generously shared with me their very personal experiences and viewpoints on life and death, for which I am extremely grateful. In a surprising number of cases I have spoken with people, some of whom have touched my life only briefly and often under bizarre circumstances.

It has been a revelation to me to discover just how many people were not only willing but appeared relieved to find an eager listener. Perhaps to talk about death removes the taboo—but who will listen?

To create a healthy balance between life and death, my belief is that we must not become so concerned with death that we forget to live, or vice versa.

Over the years I have become disillusioned by organised religion, its dogma and rigid rules. Consequently I have opted for a more individual approach, and this has taken me on a fascinating journey of self-discovery.

Having visited many places of worship and spoken to people with differing beliefs, I liken my experience to a buffet laden with food of varied flavours, textures, shapes and colours.

Preparing and sharing food has always been my way of showing people that I care. Apart from being a necessity of life, food offers comfort and reassurance, and is also a creative art. Preparing and serving food is a ceremony in itself from which great pleasures can be derived.

Following a recipe exactly has never been my style. Adding bits and pieces to the dish to give it my own personal expression has become natural. With this realisation I became aware of having an interest in all religions, but felt unable to fit into any ready-made slot.

The right food can offer immense comfort to our body; the wrong food can cause great turbulence and unrest; so it is with religion.

My basic recipe for life is 'Do unto others as you would be done by'. Flavours and seasonings added to our finished dish, or final ceremony, will reflect our soul.

ACKNOWLEDGEMENTS

I would like to thank the following people for the various ways in which they have helped me in the completion of this book.

My sincere thanks go to all those who have allowed me to share some of the most personal moments of their lives.

I am especially grateful to Janette Webber, my daughter-in-law, who has been my devil's advocate and ruthless editor. To my son Nick, daughter Carrie and her husband Brian Cort who support me wholeheartedly in all that I do. Thanks also to the members of their team at Take One Productions, especially Natasha Rooke, Dominic Cassidy and Linda Chapman.

To the Rev. Lesley Edwards BTH MA MIFC and Rev. Jacqueline Clark, Interfaith minister, for their inspirational ideas.

To Shivaun Hayes-Coles for creating order from chaos.

To all at The Natural Death Centre, my thanks for their co-operation and support.

To my team of catering helpers, I would like to express my appreciation for their loyalty and thoughtfulness.

My grateful thanks to the following people who have all contributed to the book in different ways:

The Ven. Lionel Whatley, Iain Steel, Chris Barton, Johanna & Richard Boeke, Joan Sparrow, Christine Johnson, Phil Ryan, Alex Jones, Barbara Escott, Doreen Riches, Su Lockyer, Ann Mitchell, Angela Carroll and John Russell-Milnes.

Thanks to Barbara Large without whose help and encouragement I would never have taken the first step.

Finally my thanks to all those who have supplied photographs to be used in the book, and to Charles Muller of Diadem Books who has actually made it happen.

INTRODUCTION

'Death is not the extinguishing of the light but the putting out of the lamps because the dawn has come.'

Rabindranath Tagore

Time to Go has been written as an acknowledgement that the only sure thing about life is that we shall all one day die.

Recognising that death is part of life and planning towards it can become a liberating experience. Finding a way to celebrate a special life is something many of us will be called upon to do sooner or later.

With no intention of trivialising death, the suggestions in this book are based on ideas gathered from people of many religions and cultures, embracing traditions, rituals and customs from around the world. Each scenario has a different focus.

There will never be a book that entirely removes the pain surrounding death. In spite of this, a spark of imagination can transform an otherwise sombre occasion into a joyous thanksgiving of a life, enriching the memories that live on.

Contrary to common belief, a funeral does not have to cost a fortune. Love versus costs can create an emotional tug of war often experienced when arranging a funeral. Following the shock and confusion of a sudden death, bereaved families get swept along (albeit with compassion) by possibly expensive funeral procedures, not realising the many alternative choices available. Being open-minded and daring to be different leads people to revive old traditions, where families carry out either the entire funeral or part of it themselves.

Many funeral directors are sympathetic to the need for participation, aware that personal involvement aids the grieving process. For those who wish to be in charge of their funeral, a letter containing their wishes can be prepared. This can be updated as necessary, thus removing the burden of decision making from loved ones at a traumatic and emotional time.

Arranging a funeral, which reflects the character and beliefs of the deceased, can be carried out in numerous ways. Coffins come in various forms and are made of many different materials—the biodegradable Eco Pod, willow, bamboo, cardboard and untreated pine. 'Crazy' coffins made to order in almost any design can be used, until required, as an item of furniture. Burial can take place in the back yard, orchards, fields, at sea or environmentally friendly woodland burial grounds, which have become increasingly popular, providing a haven for wildlife and an assurance that beautiful natural woodland will be available to future generations.

Experiments are currently taking place in Sweden where the body is transformed to freeze-dried granules, which are then returned to the earth. With graveyards and cemeteries full to bursting this may be a futuristic and environmentally friendly solution to the problem.

Personal touches can be introduced with flowers, music and readings, or by the choice of venue for the service or ceremony. One's imagination and the surprisingly simple guidelines set out in the pages of the *Natural Death Handbook* are the only limitations.

Ceremonies have always been used to mark important occasions in people's lives. Whilst we invest vast amounts of thought, planning and money on weddings and celebration parties, funerals generally come and go with little recognition. It is important to say goodbye in a thoughtful and meaningful way.

Whether it be mourning the tragic loss of a baby or young person, or celebrating the life of an older person who has lived life fully, grief cannot be removed—but a sensitive ceremony can ease the pain a little. It will be memories of this final act of love that will live on in people's hearts, underlining the need for a special and memorable occasion.

FUNERAL SERVICES AND CEREMONIES

Sometimes it is difficult to fund the kind of service or ceremony that reflects your beliefs, but many choices are available. There are a number of ways in which you can design your own unique ceremony. Guidance and ideas for creating the celebration of a special life are plentiful within the pages of this book.

Following Traditional Religion:

A traditional funeral involves the traditional ritual, which includes words and music that have become familiar over the centuries. Ancient and beautiful buildings have an individual charm offering the perfect place for those with a religious belief to complete the circle of life.

Interfaith Ceremonies:

Interfaith ministry is an open approach to spirituality that embraces the truth of all religions, sensitive and mindful of people's perspectives and beliefs. Ceremonies are created around what is important to you, whether your faith is traditional, or whether you have your own personally held spiritual beliefs, or have no particular beliefs of that nature; they reflect what is important to you.

Person Centred Funeral Ceremonies:

Celebrants trained by such organisations as Choice Farewells spend time getting to know the family, enabling a ceremony to be created with profound warmth and sensitivity taking into account personal beliefs and philosophies. The spiritually uplifting occasions offer an opportunity to say farewell, celebrate and give thanks for a special life in the most appropriate way.

Non-Religious Ceremonies:

For those with no religious faith, a church ceremony can be distasteful and distressing. The Humanist Society offers help with non-religious ceremonies either by providing an officiant or by giving advice and help to families who wish to carry out such a ceremony themselves.

'Do It Yourself' Ceremonies:

An increasing number of people are becoming aware of their own individual spirituality, feeling unable to fit into conventional slots. Creating a heartfelt ceremony delivered by the family can be a personal and loving touch. For those who find it difficult to express their grief publicly, a celebrant will co-ordinate and articulate thoughts and feelings on their behalf.

Civil Funeral Ceremonies:

A civil funeral ceremony reflects the wishes of the family and is focused on celebrating the life of the deceased. Created by a professional celebrant in consultation with the family or executor, the ceremony can take place anywhere except in churches or religious buildings. It is appropriate for either cremation or burial at any non-religious burial ground.

NATURAL HARMONY

With her health deteriorating, Jo made plans for her own Green funeral, with a willow coffin garlanded with sweet scented roses. An envelope containing a special memory and a gift for each friend became part of the spiritual ceremony led by an independent Minister where cake and wine were shared at the graveside.

<u>Introduction</u>

Jo had no immediate family and she was anxious not to be a burden on anybody when death came. Having lived her life independently, her desire to leave the same way was strong. From articles she had read and people she had spoken to she gathered ideas. Jo began to plan her funeral in a way whereby she could express herself and her love for her many friends.

Jo had no fear of death, having experienced a near death experience (NDE) during an operation many years before. She had told few people about this life-changing incident. During the operation Jo had left her body. Looking down with detachment, she had watched doctors trying to resuscitate her. She travelled down a long tunnel with a bright light at the end and; having had a brief glimpse of what comes after death, she was told that it was not yet her time and that she should return to her body.

Arrangements

Having made some basic decisions, Jo searched the internet for information on woodland burial grounds. She:

- Visited and reserved a plot at her chosen place belonging to the Association of Nature Reserve Burial Grounds. She received two copies of the deed of ownership, invoices and receipt.
- Discussed details with funeral directors familiar with Green burial; chose her coffin and confirmed a pre-paid funeral plan.
- Contacted 'Choice Farewells' to discuss the contents of a non-religious ceremony.
- Completed a Living Will Form and a Form of Advance Funeral Wishes.

Jo discovered a new found freedom and inner strength, having discussed the details of her ceremony with the highly recommended celebrant and filled in a pre-funeral plan. She gave copies of all the documents to a solicitor who was also to act as her executor and who she knew would carry out her wishes. When the time came and Jo knew she was soon going to die, she evaluated the plans she had made earlier and decided she would also like to become a participant at her own funeral.

Coffin

Jo chose a woven willow coffin, and when placing the order she requested that stalks of lavender be woven into the willow. The sides were to be garlanded with sweet scented roses, stephanotis and rosemary for remembrance—the fragrance would undoubtedly be intoxicating.

<u>Flowers</u>	Jo's travels in India and her experiences there led her to request that rather than flowers, any donations be made to the deserving charity 'Wells for India' which works towards making clean water—the source of all life—available for everyone.
<u>Location</u>	The place Jo chose for her burial had been pasture until an outbreak of Foot and Mouth occurred. Now a Green burial site, the grass will be mown two or three times a year encouraging wild flowers to set their seeds. Trees planted will develop eventually into natural woodland, each one marking a grave. A small area is set aside with a seat for quiet contemplation. Jo chose this place as it would require no upkeep, she knew she could rest undisturbed and her body would return to nature in a beautiful setting.
<u>Service/ Ceremony</u>	The Celebrant was standing beside Jo's coffin in the tranquil setting as friends gathered at the graveside. Dusk would fall within the hour.
	Having lived in Greece for several years, Jo chose to adopt a local custom of breaking cake and sharing wine at the graveside.
	When Jo knew she was dying she prepared an envelope for each of her friends who had been the jewels in her life; the envelopes were distributed at the graveside by the Celebrant, each one containing a small gift. Shared memories were read aloud with anecdotes and messages. Mourners lit candles and stood around the grave. As night fell the candles twinkled like stars; musicians, a short distance away, played.
<u>Refreshments</u>	Snatches of gracious living had been enjoyed regularly by Jo and her friends taking tea at a country house hotel, on the lawns in summer and by cosy log fires in

winter. This would be her last opportunity to act as hostess to her friends.

Memorial

A tree native to the area was planted over the grave the following autumn. This single contribution promised a sense of continuity to what would one day become a beautiful natural woodland.

Reflections

Her friends agreed that Jo's passing had taken place with great dignity, just as she had planned.

Notes:

- Woodland burial grounds search www.naturaldeath.org.uk
- Donations were made to Wells for India, a charity close to Jo's heart. Tel: 01962 848043.
- The ceremony was created and conducted by Choice Farewells. Tel: 023 8086 1256; www.choicefarewells.co.uk
- Living Will Forms and Forms of Advance Funeral Wishes are available from The Natural Death Centre. Tel: 0871 288 2098; www.naturaldeath.org.uk
- Somerset Willow Coffins. Tel: 01278 424003.

DOWN TO EARTH

Having the courage to be different led the family to organise the funeral themselves. A cardboard coffin covered in memorabilia was carried through the village, led by a jazz band and buried at a simple ceremony in a wild flower meadow.

Introduction

It was Lewis's choice and a family decision that he be brought home from hospital and allowed to die naturally. His wife Sarah had received nursing training; her memories of death on the ward had been ones of hushed silence, but she now had the opportunity to express her thoughts and feelings regarding natural death. With the aid of information and guidance from The Natural Death Center, the couple discussed their fears surrounding death, sharing many thoughts and feelings. As Lewis became weaker, he decided to abstain from food, drinking only juices and eventually just water. He finally died in Sarah's arms with his family around him. They telephoned the Doctor who confirmed the cause of death and issued a certificate, which was taken to the Registrar. Sarah washed her husband's body in lavender water before laying him out. Assistance from friends came in many forms; they helped transfer Lewis's body to the cold garage, arranging ice packs around him until the final arrangements were complete.

Arrangements   The couple had witnessed many impersonal funerals and had experienced cold detachment from funeral directors in the past, which made them decide to carry out the arrangements themselves.

Coffin   The children spent time in their father's room choosing photographs and reminiscing. Lewis helped select the ones they glued onto the cardboard coffin. A collage of memorabilia, messages, verses, pressed flowers, trinkets and treasures were also added. Creating this work of art had given the siblings a feeling of participation.

On the morning of the funeral Lewis's body was placed into the beautifully decorated coffin and surrounded by cushions full of shredded paper to keep his body in place. Sarah had previously ordered a wicker stretcher on which the cardboard coffin would be supported.

Flowers   Small posies of garden flowers were made and arranged around the coffin, forming a montage of colour.

Transport   Four friends acted as bearers to Lewis's now featherweight body, which was carried from their home, through the village and past the Six Crowns to his final resting place.

Location

Provided no financial exchange took place and with the landowner's permission, Lewis was to be buried in a meadow. (See Appendix Two).

It was Sarah's wish to be buried beside her husband when the time came. A group of young friends dug the grave in the chalky hillside that had previously been farmland from which a beautiful wild flower meadow had been created.

By arrangement with the landlord of the village pub, which had been Lewis's local, mourners met and parked in the car park. Led by the jazz band of which Lewis had been the lead trombonist, he was carried through the village and marched to his grave within a procession consisting of all those who loved him. A lark sang high in the summer sky as they reached the beautiful meadow—part of the living landscape of which Lewis would become part.

Service/ Ceremony

The bearers placed the coffin on the scaffold boards which covered the grave. A short and sensitive ceremony followed conducted by Lewis's nearest and dearest.

- Prayers were said thanking God for Lewis's life and love, which included the Lord's Prayer.
- The band played 'Abide With Me'.
- A few moments of personal reflection were observed.
- The coffin was slowly lowered on strips of webbing with two people on either side into its final resting place.
- Everyone tossed wild flowers from the meadow into the grave. Those who wished to do so helped replace the soil as the band played a selection of their friend's favourite pieces.

- Before leaving, handfuls of wild flower seeds natural to the area were scattered on the grave—harebells, scabious, lady's slipper, buttercups and cowslips.

Refreshments   Drinks and memories were shared at the pub on the way back to the family home where a cold fork buffet was waiting. Many people had found a part to play preparing a feast of delicious eats for the homecoming.

Memorial   Sarah planted a flowering almond tree in the garden, which would bloom every year on Lewis's birthday. So that he would never be forgotten, the family planned to meet every year on this day.

Carrying out the funeral themselves was not about cost-cutting so much as ethics. Sarah commissioned a play system, hand crafted in wood for the children's school playground with the money she had saved. This was dedicated to Lewis's memory at a short ceremony.

Reflections   Nursing her husband at home until his death gave Sarah a feeling of peace. She was thankful that he had not suffered for long. Sharing their marital bed, being close to one another until the end had been such a comfort, an experience unheard of on a hospital ward. The family involvement had taught the children that death is a natural part of life, something to be celebrated.

Notes:

- Sarah and Lewis had both read the book *Who Dies?* by Stephen Levine; it had helped them with the concept of natural death.
- For information on burial on private land, see Appendix Two.

- The cost of the funeral had been minimal; a cardboard coffin with fluid proof liner, wicker stretcher and webbing had been their only expense. All available from Heaven on Earth. Tel: 0117 926 4999.
- Wild flower seeds—genetically approved from Flora Naturescape; Tel: 01949 860592.
- *The Natural Death Handbook*. Tel: 0871 288 2098.
- Wildwood Playgrounds: Tel:01293 851597; www.wildwood-playgrounds.com

BETH'S GOODBYE

Disharmony between two sisters regarding their mother's funeral arrange-ments ultimately led to the creation of a special ceremony of farewell to loved ones and the family home.

<u>Introduction</u> Holding joint power of attorney and with little com-munication between them, the two sisters Beth and Lindsay found that many problems arose. Beth would not have known of the death of their widowed mother, Alwyn, had the hospital not notified both sis-ters. Lindsay, being the eldest, took responsibility for the funeral arrangements and was unwilling to discuss them with her sister. Following the service of commit-tal Beth was horrified and embarrassed that a gather-ing afterwards for family and friends had not been arranged.

Arrangements

Several months after Alwyn's funeral Beth shared her grief and hurt with a friend who suggested she contacted Choice Farewells which specialises in the creation of ceremonies for the milestones of life.

Beth and the Celebrant met at the family home where her parents and latterly her mum alone had lived for sixty-five years, now empty, cold and dejected with a FOR SALE board outside. Beth prepared to say 'goodbye' to all that had been dear to her.

Ceremony

It was a beautiful day, and those who wished to accept Beth's invitation were there to take part. Holding a lighted candle, the celebrant led the group around the house, sharing their memories, both happy and sad as they went, placing flowers and lighting a candle in each room. When the nostalgic tour was complete, everybody gathered in the garden for a prayer. 'The Dream of Alwyn' played as they wrote a short message on labels attached to biodegradable balloons, which were then released into the blue sky, representing freedom as Alwyn's spirit moved on.

Refreshments

Mum's best china and tableware were used as everyone enjoyed tea in the garden (which included strawberries and cream) as they had on so many past occasions. They also drank to Mum's life with her homemade wine from the larder.

Memorial

Everybody wrote a message or memory in a special book made of handmade paper. Beth wrote the following:

Farewell to Alwyn and Ken and their home
'To love and to be loved is to live forever.'

A photographic record of the family house from the day her parents moved in has since been added.

Reflection

Beth realised how easily relatives could be offended by exclusion; this experience also severely increased the effect of bereavement. Her mother had made a will but had not written down her funeral wishes. To have done so would have spared much of her daughter's trauma. Beth felt happy to have finally found a way of celebrating the life of her parents and 'letting go' of the family home.

Notes:

- The ceremony was created and conducted by Choice Farewells.
  Tel: 023 8086 1256; www.choiceceremonies.co.uk
- Biodegradable balloons available from balloon suppliers. See Yellow Pages.

BLACK LACE

A Roman Catholic funeral service with mass for an elderly lady who always respected her appearance was followed by cremation. Her ashes were later interred in her husband's grave.

Introduction

Having always taken a great pride in her appearance, Nora had now reached an age when her body had begun to wear out though she still felt young at heart. Since her husband's death she had lived in a rest home, condensing her home into one small room and managing now with the support of carers. Members of her large Catholic family were at her bedside while tapes of her favourite music played as she lay near death. Letting go of her rosary she began to fumble frantically in her handbag, anxious to find her lipstick, smiling at the photograph of her husband beside her. "I can't meet him without my lipstick," she said in a hushed whisper. The Priest came to give her the last rites as she literally let go. Her carer placed a flower on the pillow beside her and said a personal prayer.

Arrangements

Funeral directors recommended by the rest home took charge of the arrangements. Nora's records confirmed her intention to be cremated, and also that she wished to look especially attractive for her last day on earth. The Embalmer ensured that her make-up and hair were perfect; with the aid of a photograph they re-created the attractive woman she had been. Together, the family prepared the liturgy for the service, which provided consolation for them within their mourning.

Coffin

Mass cards were displayed at the funeral home where Nora lay in her open coffin wearing a black negligée, looking young and beautiful. Relatives gathered to view the body, sitting with bowed heads in silent prayer.

Flowers

Extravagant floral tributes and sympathy cards were received by the funeral directors who displayed them later at the crematorium. On the coffin from the immediate family was the word 'MUM' worked in flower heads.

Location

Following the evening service, Nora's coffin was received into the church where a short service of prayers and music took place. The evening sun shone through the stained glass windows and bathed the scene with vibrant colours. The assembled choir consisted of a number of Nora's friends—retired parishioners from the village.

**Service/
Ceremony**

The church bells rang out and sacred music was played on the organ as mourners took their places of familiar comfort in church.

- The service focused on the mystery of the death and resurrection of Christ and was interspersed with Nora's best loved religious music.
- Favourite scripture readings, psalms and prayers were recited.
- Memories were recalled by a family friend with a focus on Nora's Irish charm and cheerful nature.
- Nora's grandchildren delivered the bread and wine to the altar for communion.
- Celebration of the funeral liturgy took place.
- The service ended with 'The Song of Farewell'.

Older mourners wore black as a mark of respect and a number of elderly gentlemen doffed their hats and bowed as the hearse took Nora on the final stage of her journey.

Prayers led by the Priest at the crematorium were brief; only the closest family members attended the committal.

Refreshments Relatives came together from far and wide, contributing food for the gathering, which presented a natural excuse for a get-together and included plenty of Nora's favourite tipple.

Memorial
- Nora's ashes were later interred in her husband's grave at the cemetery.
- A mass was planned for the anniversary of her death.
- A garden seat was placed in Nora's favourite spot in the garden at the rest home. Commissioned by the family, it was made to a unique design, using locally grown oak and sweet chestnut. The inscription on the back read:

A kiss of the sun for pardon,
The song of the birds for mirth
You are nearer God's heart in a garden
Than anywhere else on earth.

By Dorothy Frances Gurney

Reflections   Recalling Nora's preparations for her departure, the family realised death is not necessarily a time of separation and loss but of expectation and reconciliation.

While sorting out Nora's possessions, a crumpled bag containing baby's bootees, first teeth and locks of hair were discovered. The family regretted not sending these treasures with their mother who had kept them for so many years.

Notes: The garden seat was designed and made by The Stile Company, Tel: 01295 780372.

BLUEBELL WOODS

An ecological woodland burial with a religious graveside service. Buried in her wedding dress, Julie had a bamboo coffin. A bush marked her grave, later to be replaced by a tree when her husband would occupy the other half.

<u>Introduction</u>   Julie and George had been blessed with a short but romantic marriage. Their courtship had begun when they made love amongst the bluebells one sunny May day. Life had continued happily until news of Julie's condition was revealed. George knew that therapy would prolong his wife's life long enough to enable them to concentrate their minds on priorities and settle their affairs. They were grateful for this opportunity and glad they had not been given false hope. Speaking often of being together again, they expressed their love for one another and accepted Julie's death calmly.

Arrangements

George and Julie visited the beautiful Green woodland burial ground they had chosen, which was managed ecologically, providing an informal nature-rich environment. The burial centre works alongside the client's chosen funeral director, welcoming people of all beliefs. Together, George and Julie chose a plot for a double grave, checking the longevity of the site; they also discussed the requirements of Green burial; the use of resin, embalming fluids or chemicals was forbidden in order to maintain an ecological environment. Having paid a deposit to secure the plot, they received the deed of ownership and George agreed on monthly payments.

Coffin

A number of biodegradable, non-toxic coffins were on display at the centre. Julie chose a Bamboo Eco Coffin with woven handles and threaded lid-fastenings, and a resting-place that could not be more natural. She wished to be buried in her wedding dress, which she and George felt would be appropriate.

When the time came, George visited Julie at the chapel of rest. As she lay in her wedding dress, he placed a red rose in her hands with a love letter and a photograph of them both on their wedding day.

Transport

The Funeral Directors drove Julie's body to the woodland burial site where George said his private goodbye before mourners arrived.

Location

Everyone gathered in the Sustainability Centre for coffee, where Julie's coffin, delicately interwoven with wild flowers, now lay on a wooden bier. The Minister who had married the couple said a few words before guiding the procession towards a chorus of sweet voices that echoed through the woodland—a group of the couples' friends belonging to a choir had joined together for the occasion. George, supported by several friends, wheeled the bier himself along the narrow woodland pathways to the graveside. A four-wheel-drive vehicle was available to transport elderly mourners unable to manage the walk.

**Service/
Ceremony**

- The service began with readings from the Bible.
- Everyone joined the choir and sang 'Where E'er You Walk' by Handel from his opera 'Semele'.
- Prayers and psalms were said.
- A single male voice sang 'The Lake Isle of Innisfree' by W B Yeats, set to music by Andrew Usher.
- A friend recited a traditional Irish blessing:
  May the road rise with you,
  May the wind be always at your back.
  May the sun shine warm upon your face,
  May the rain fall soft upon your fields,
  And until we meet again—
  May God hold you in the hollow of his hands.
- The Minister spoke of Julie and George's loving marriage, their close connections with the church and Julie's calm acceptance and courage following her illness. He praised the couple for the way in which together they had prepared for this day and their eventual reunion.
- Julie's coffin was lowered into her resting-place with the traditional words being said: "Earth to earth, ashes to ashes, dust to dust".
- Everyone joined the choir and sang 'O For the Wings of a Dove' by Mendelssohn.

- On their wedding day Julie and George had released a pair of doves—a symbol of peace. The ritual was repeated on this occasion, and as the birds soared into the blue sky they took Julie's spirit with them.

Refreshments

Following the service everyone gathered at a quaint, country pub for refreshments

Memorial

Microchip technology marked the grave and a bush would also be planted on the site. A tree could then take its place following George's eventual burial—a living alternative to a headstone. In no time the grave would be covered with wild flowers native to the countryside. By mail-order George sent for Hyacinthoides Non-Scripta (genetically approved bluebells) which added his own personal signature to nature's abundance.

A photograph of Julie and some chosen words were placed in the memorial book displayed at the Centre.

Reflections

George took comfort in having played an active role in his wife's funeral and from the fact that they had been given the opportunity to choose a place of stillness and seclusion where they could eventually be together again.

Notes:

- To help fill the gap left in his own life, George eventually involved himself in voluntary work.
- He accepted counselling which was offered by his church.
- Bamboo Eco Coffins are available from funeral directors or direct: Tel: 01795 472262.
- Genetically approved Flora Naturescape: Tel:01949 860592
- The White Dove Company: Tel: 020 8502 2461 www.thewhitedovecompany.co.uk

BOB THE BUILDER

Humour had always been Bob's trademark. Being agnostic, a non-religious funeral service was conducted by a Humanist Officiant. Bob had always maintained that he was walked over in life, so his ashes were made into a stepping stone for the garden.

Introduction   When their father retired from the family construction business, Bob and Mick became directors. Their employees, 'the lads', were linked as a team at work and by friendship. An indication of the humorous environment in which they worked was the important notice in the store:

'The Management regret that it has come to their attention that Employees dying on the job are failing to fall down. This practice must stop as it becomes impossible to distinguish between Death and natural movement of the staff. Any Employee found dead in an upright position will be dropped from the payroll.—Managing Director.'

The living nightmare began when Sue received news of her husband's sudden death following an accident. Stunned and unable to believe the news, she was grateful to 'the lads' who gave whatever help they could to her and the children.

Arrangements

The Funeral Directors were agreeable to the family carrying out some of the arrangements themselves. Mick was on holiday and could not be contacted for some time. The Funeral Directors collected Bob's body from the hospital and also dealt with the statutory authorities, leaving the family free to plan the more personal aspects of the occasion.

An officiant from the British Humanist Association was contacted who explained a non-religious ceremony to Sue and Mick, offering advice where required. Whilst not wishing to demean death in any way, they were anxious that Bob's humour was reflected in the occasion. Together they created a service with which they were pleased and hoped everyone present would approve. They agreed to supply their own music CDs.

Coffin

'The lads' were anxious to make Bob's coffin themselves, using recycled oak floorboards which would be natural and solid like 'the boss'. They checked with the crematorium which issued them with an information sheet: the coffin had to be made of suitable material for combustion to avoid unnecessary pollution. They also checked the size. When complete, the coffin was taken to the funeral directors and Bob's body was placed inside. 'The lads' attached a plate bearing Bob's details. Hammering in the nails to fix the lid was all part of their personal therapy.

<u>Flowers</u>	Flowers were delivered in many shapes and forms, which were arranged around the coffin. Sue's special tribute was a heart-shaped cushion of red roses.
<u>Transport</u>	Bob's coffin was collected from the Funeral Directors in the firm's pick-up truck, which had been cleaned and polished for the occasion. Surrounded by flowers, it was reverently driven to the crematorium by Mick, keeping to the strict crematorium time schedule.
<u>Location</u>	Being a non-religious service, the altar cross was removed and the space filled with flowers for the duration of the service. Bob's coffin was carefully shouldered into the chapel, defiantly feet first by Mick and five of 'the lads' to a CD playing: 'He Ain't Heavy, He's My Brother'. Jeans and T-shirts were the dress of the day, which was an expression of Bob's relaxed ways.
<u>Service/</u> <u>Ceremony</u>	The service was carefully timed to twenty minutes and began with the Officiant introducing himself, giving the reasons why a non-religious service was fulfilling Bob's thoughts on life and death and that he hoped mourners would not find the idea disrespectful in any way. He went on to explain that a time of quiet would be provided for personal prayer during the service.

- The tribute focused on Bob being a husband, son, father, team leader, and a practical man, remembering him as he was, in sadness for his death but in appreciation for his life and for his wonderful humour.
- Everyone stood for the committal while 'Stairway to Heaven' by Led Zeppelin played and the curtain drew around the coffin.
- A time for personal prayer was observed.

- The Officiant's closing words were to mention the arrangements for refreshments and to thank everyone on behalf of the family for coming, he added, "and keep up the support."
- The final piece of music played as mourners departed was 'Knocking on Heaven's Door' by Bob Dylan.

Refreshments

Everyone gathered at the pub for a pie and a pint, which was what Bob would have liked.

Reflections

At a time of such distress, discretion had been difficult; but in spite of her anxiety, Sue did not wish to offend anybody by not having a religious service, especially Bob's aged parents. The Humanist ceremony had conveyed a deep and personal meaning, which fulfilled the requirement perfectly.

Memorial

Keeping Bob's memory alive, the lads mixed his ashes with concrete, which they made into a stepping stone for the garden. This was inscribed with the invitation: 'Go on, walk all over me!'

Notes:

- After the funeral Sue felt angry with Bob for leaving her to bring up their family alone. She realised the best way to come to terms with her grief was to discuss it and find ways to release her anger. A leaflet in the doctor's waiting room led her to a bereavement counsellor from whom she and the children (who did not attend the funeral) received much support.
- The ceremony was written and conducted by a celebrant from The British Humanist Association. Tel: 020 7430 0908; www.humanism.org.uk.

DEEP TO DEEP

A dramatic sea burial at sunset, followed by a champagne and canapé reception at a maritime museum. The conditions of her children's inheritance were dependent upon Rachael's wishes being carried out.

Introduction   Rachael's father and husband had both been buried at sea during active service and Rachael made elaborate arrangements so that when it was her turn she could join her loved ones. Her own connections with the RAF during the war had had a major impact on her view of life and she had maintained many links. Rachael's relationship with her adult children and their families had become estranged; consequently she took responsibility for her own funeral arrangements. All the necessary information required to carry out her instructions was lodged with her will in the hands of her solicitor.

Arrangements

The tradition of burial at sea is an ancient one. Rachael realised it was a complicated and expensive option. Being aware that her children may choose to overlook her requests, the conditions of their inheritance depended upon her wishes being carried out.

Rachael approached a Funeral Director specialising in sea burial who, following the guidelines set out by the Department for the Environment and Rural Affairs (DEFRA), explained the complexity and cost of the arrangements. The price she was finally given included the hire of a boat and its crew.

When the day dawned the Funeral Directors obtained the necessary licence and certificates; they also placed notices in the appropriate newspapers regarding Rachael's funeral arrangements.

Coffin

Rachael's coffin, complying with regulations, was made of soft wood, substantially strengthened and weighted, with holes drilled in the sides and bottom so that the coffin might sink rapidly. Flexible steel strappings ensured its safe deposit on the sea bed. Regulations stated that the coffin should contain no persistent plastics, copper or zinc; nor must the body be embalmed—just wrapped loosely in a cotton sheet with an identification tag attached to the body (in the unlikely case of its being washed ashore).

Flowers

Wreaths were to be cast into the sea; some were made of flowers, some of laurel leaves—a symbol of victory.

Transport

The Funeral Director delivered Rachael's coffin to the dock where it was winched aboard the awaiting craft.

<u>Vessel</u>	As set out by DEFRA, the vessel fulfilled the requirements of adequate navigational equipment, the Master was suitably qualified and the weather conditions were agreeable.
	Mourners were piped aboard as the Captain and Chaplain welcomed and escorted them to the cabin for refreshments. With the coffin firmly secured and covered by a union jack, they set out to sea.
<u>Service/ Ceremony</u>	Upon reaching the designated burial area the colours were lowered to half-mast. An RAF Chaplain, known to Rachael, conducted a short service during which he said a prayer of committal as the coffin was lowered into the water and consumed by the waves. As the piper played a lament, mourners cast their wreaths into the sea, and the wreaths merged with the reflected colours of the beautiful sunset. A passing ship's crew removed their hats in respect and dipped their ensign.
<u>Reception</u>	The 'Onedin Line' was being played by the piper as mourners stepped ashore and were taken the short distance by taxi to a champagne and canapé reception at a maritime museum. The Chaplain on behalf of the family thanked everyone for attending and for the letters of condolence received by the family. He went on to read from a card the words by Bishop Brent:

What is Dying?

A ship sails and I stand watching till she fades on the horizon and someone at my side says "she is gone".

Gone where? Gone from my sight, that is all, she is just as large as when I saw her. The diminished size, and total loss of sight is in me, not in her, and just at the moment when someone at my side says "She is gone" there are others who are watching her coming and other voices take up a glad shout, "There she comes!" and that is dying.

<u>Reflections</u>

Until Rachael's death was announced, her family had no idea what sort of funeral she had wanted. They carried out their mother's wishes but they felt that to have scattered her ashes at sea, which required no permission, would have been a simpler and cheaper solution.

Notes:

- Rachael had written her own obituary.
- The right weather conditions are vital for burial at sea. The day and time of the service can be postponed for 24 hours, if the captain feels conditions are too rough.
- Sea burials can only take place in three areas around the British coast:
  The Needles, Isle of Wight;
  Newhaven;
  Northumberland.

Specialists in sea burial:

- The British Shipping Company.
  Tel: 01395 568652.
  (or any reputable funeral director)
- The Piper, James Wilde. Tel: 01903 266994.

FAREWELL TO JOSH

Josh lay in a tiny walnut cradle on a bed of flowers for his naming ritual. The non-religious ceremony included a goodnight story read by his parents before he was cremated. Everyone lit a candle in his memory.

Introduction The result of the post-mortem examination was registered as Sudden Infant Death Syndrome (SIDS). A CID Officer visited Gary and Emma's home to ask questions and gather information. This formality was, not surprisingly, extremely distressing for them. Twelve days earlier the couple had left hospital with two healthy babies, Alice and Josh. Following her brother's death, Alice underwent a full medical examination and was deemed fit and well. Initially Emma and Gary could not believe what had happened; this was followed by shock, bewilderment, and overwhelming feelings of guilt. The 24-hour helpline of the Foundation for the Study of Infant Deaths was very supportive of them. The couple's faith helped them initially, but this began to waiver when they approached their priest asking him to baptise Josh. They were devastated to learn that he felt unable to christen a dead baby.

To Emma and Gary it was incredibly important that their son was acknowledged as a real entity; a part of them and their family giving a feeling of connectedness with his soul and the divine.

Arrangements

Emma learned from a friend about a Celebrant trained by Choice Farewells who would carry out a naming ritual for Josh. The Celebrant visited the family home to discuss the funeral service, which would begin with a naming ritual. Together they compiled a ceremony, sending a copy to the funeral director who in turn booked a double slot at the crematorium which would allow time for preparing and clearing the chapel. Emma and Gary felt comforted that in their hearts Josh would be in the care of God in spite of his rejection by the Church.

Coffin

Emma recalled reading in a book on archaeology about a tiny baby's remains being found laid on a swan's wing, wrapped in rushes; this information had touched her heart. The thought of having to choose a container for Josh's tiny body devastated her until she was informed by the Funeral Director of a newly designed little 'walnut cradle'. Made from recycled paper with a feather lining and overlaid with hand-made mulberry and silk paper, tied at the sides with ribbons, this felt comfortable and right. Toys that had been gifts to Josh were tucked beside him.

<u>Flowers</u>	Rather than formal floral tributes, mourners carried armfuls of flowers that formed a bed on which the tiny walnut cradle would rest.
<u>Transport</u>	The family collected the little coffin from the funeral directors. Gary also wanted to carry his son into the crematorium himself.
<u>Location</u>	A double slot having been booked at the crematorium avoided the feeling of being rushed. The Celebrant had discussed with the management a wish to use candles in the ceremony. This was agreed, providing collars were used to avoid any wax stains.
<u>Service/ Ceremony</u>	Having prepared a table covered by a delicate cloth, the Celebrant created a beautiful bed of flowers on which Gary carefully arranged the walnut cradle. Schubert's 'Ave Maria' was played on CD as mourners took their places.

The celebrant began the service with the words:

- "A candle being lit as a symbol that this little one has lived and that life, however fleeting, has been precious."
- The naming ceremony continued as the Celebrant spoke about a name being related to the soul and names carrying with them the essence of a child's identity. "Joshua Taylor" (water was poured onto the walnut cradle as each of his names were spoken).
- "Joshua we give you your first name, a name from the cradle of the world, for Joshua means 'the world of salvation'. Joshua Taylor, we give you the surname as an important name full of history; you take it with you as a tender bearer of your past. Joshua Taylor, you are part of your family for ever."

- The Celebrant continued to speak of the twelve precious days when Josh's personality had unfolded itself to the family.
- She spoke about the signs and symbols of life, water being the source of all life; salt being the element of the earth and sea, tears and in our blood; and Oil being light energy and healing.
- The Celebrant began Joshua Taylor's farewell by acknowledging the pain in the hearts of his parents and grandparents and those who shared so much hope in this new life and of Alice who mirrors her twin's suffering; and of others close to the family.
- A poem adapted for the occasion was read by Emma's sister.
- The Celebrant then lit a candle from a main candle as a reminder that Josh is like the tumbling of the stars, reflecting deeply within our hearts.
- The ceremony continued with Emma and Gary reading in turn to Josh their goodnight story. 'Guess How Much I Love You' by Sam Mc Bratney.
- The Celebrant then requested that everyone help recreate the bed of flowers on the catafalque so that Gary may lay Josh down to rest.
- The Celebrant continued: "Josh, in his walnut cradle moves on to his final resting place" as 'Fly' (Celine Dion's beautiful song) played.
- Following a few closing words, the curtain drew and everyone lit candles on the way out as 'A Long Day is Over' was played on CD.

Refreshments   Food had been the last thing on Emma's mind but it had been a helpful therapy for her mother to make these arrangements. Everybody hugged one another with few words being spoken for sometime.

Before leaving, everyone signed a special book and wrote loving messages as a keepsake for Emma and Gary.

Memorial

As a living memorial to Josh, several family members decided to sponsor a child in an underdeveloped country through the charity 'Plan'. They also decided that on Josh and Alice's birthday every year they would light a symbolic candle especially for Josh.

Reflections

In spite of their grief and dashed dreams, the family found that the funeral service and ritual involved had been a healing experience. The acknowledgement that Josh always would be a special human being and an important part of the family before letting him go was a significant milestone in their recovery.

Notes:

- The parents were warned that following the cremation process of an infant there would probably be no tangible remains left.

- Emma and Gary's love of God remains, but their spirituality has changed since their devastating experience with the church.

- A year had passed; Emma's grief was hard to overcome. She felt people were talking about her behind her back, and felt she had to prove her innocence. She contacted the League of Compassionate Friends (LCF) who offer support to bereaved families. This resulted in her meeting people with whom she had a common bond and Emma felt able to talk truly and honestly about her feelings. Tel: 0117 966 5202; www.tcf.org.uk

- The ceremony was written and conducted by the founder of Choice Ceremonies. Tel: 023 8086 1256; www.choiceceremonies.co.uk
- The Foundation for the Study of Infant Death (FSID). 24 hour help line: Tel: 020 7233 2090.
- To sponsor a child in an undeveloped country. Plan. Tel: 020 7482 9777; www.plan-uk.org
- Walnut cradle by Arka Ecopod. Tel: 01273 746011. Email: hazel@ecopod.co.uk www.ecopod.co.uk

FINAL MILESTONE

Having Aids highlighted Ben's friendships. His pre-planned funeral embraced their various religions, traditions and customs. His 'crazy coffin' was cremated during an Interfaith service. A ceremony was organised by his friends during which his ashes were strewn in a lake, a ceremony that included lighted candles in origami boats. A shared meal followed which incorporated dishes of the world.

Introduction

Ben had gambled with life in the past, and now accepted that he was terminally ill and that he had only one year to live. He planned this time thoughtfully, taking a holiday while he was still able, and arranged his funeral.

Ben found Death Tutoring consoling but realised it would not change his destiny; the Counsellor encouraged him to talk about what he expected would happen when death came.

During his lifetime he often felt that few people understood him, especially his family. He knew all about loneliness and abandonment, and he took this opportunity to record his feelings on videotape, which enabled him to heal the rift with his family.

Arrangements   Ben began to arrange his funeral in the supportive atmosphere of the hospice to which he moved as he became weaker, exchanging ideas and thoughts with others around him. In view of the mixed religious beliefs to which he had been exposed, he decided on a ceremony conducted by an Interfaith minister whose ministry would embrace all religions. The Minister helped Ben plan a sensitive and personal celebration of his life.

Ben took out a pre-paid funeral plan and gave the flexible funeral directors a copy of his letter of wishes, which included hygienic embalming.

Coffin   Happy memories flooded back of a holiday spent with friends when he saw an illustration of a canal boat coffin. He took delight in placing an order and he could also enjoy its decorative effects meanwhile. He checked with the manufacturer that the materials would be acceptable for cremation.

Flowers   Ben requested that there be no flowers at his funeral but that any donations should be made directly to the hospice where he had received so much support.

Transport   Ben arranged with a friend that when the time came he would be towed in his canal boat to the crematorium on a boat trailer.

Location   A double slot at an extra charge had been booked at the crematorium as several of his friends wished to make contributions to the service; this also allowed time for setting up a video player. A special request that candles be used had been granted by the crematorium manager providing no wax was spilled; cardboard collars were used to avoid any damage.

**Service/
Ceremony**

Printed on the front of the service sheet:

> *Even as water becomes one with water, fire with fire and air with air, so the mind becomes one with the infinite mind and thus attains final freedom.*

Ben's crazy coffin was shouldered into the chapel by six friends of a similar height and placed on the catafalque as 'Aum Nama Sivaya' played on the CD.

- Wearing a stole bearing the religious symbols of the world, the Minister welcomed mourners to the ceremony in which Ben's life would be celebrated and honoured. She explained that Ben wanted this to be a time of reconciliation where any relationships that had been less than perfect during this lifetime could be healed.

- A reading by friend Sally—'Crossing the Bar' by Alfred Lord Tennyson. The Minister continued to explain why the creation of this special service was so important to Ben.

- Having lived life to the full, Ben had many friends of different religions and not having his roots in any particular faith he believed there were many paths to the Divine and that all were valid. To show the importance of his friendships the creation of this ceremony draws on the writings and traditions of different faiths.

- On the table, in the Buddhist tradition, stood a photograph of Ben, which was cremated with him.

- Offerings of food, a stick of incense, flowers and some candles are from Ben's Buddhist friend Jane who lit the candles and incense and recited a Buddhist text.

- Ben's Jewish friend, Eliyahu, led everyone in reciting together the 23rd psalm.
- Ben's Hindu friend Soni read the Hindu prayer for peace.
- The video of Ben's eulogy was played.
- A candle-lighting ceremony then took place where the flame was passed from candle to candle, the end candle in each row being lit from a taper.
- A few moments were taken for private goodbyes to Ben, a Tibetan bowl being rung at the beginning and end of the short period of silence.
- A prayer was said giving thanks for shared memories and tribute paid to the gifts that Ben had brought into many lives.
- Everyone stood for the committal.
- Candles were blown out as those present let Ben go; the light of peace welcomed Ben as he began his homeward journey.
- Closing reading.
- Blessing.
- 'Sailing', by Rod Stewart, played on CD as mourners made their exit saying farewell to Ben in whatever way was appropriate to them.

When everyone had departed from the chapel the curtains drew around the coffin and candles were carefully extinguished. Ben's two closest friends felt that by witnessing the committal of the body into the flames, the finality of the act would help them with their grieving.

Refreshments   An Indian family with whom Ben had spent many happy hours had prepared a curry meal at home to which everyone was welcomed. They shared food and memories and told stories, happy and sad, well into the night.

An idea developed during the evening, which had not been part of Ben's plan. His friends decided to create a special occasion at which to scatter his ashes in a beautiful and sensitive ceremony; this would include customs from many countries. They checked with his next of kin that this would be appropriate and invited any family members who wished to attend.

Memorial Celebration

Everyone gathered in the park beside the lake at dusk as three violins played Handel's 'Water Music'.

Customs were adopted from many countries:

- Asian friends lit tiny candles that were placed into biodegradable origami boats, each one holding a special message for Ben. The candles eventually burnt out, taking with them the messages.
- The Hindus wore white, their traditional colour of mourning.
- Romanian friends sang and danced, as is their tradition.
- Garlands of marigolds, traditional herbs of healing, were worn around the necks of western friends.
- The Chinese distributed candy for good luck.

Refreshments

After the celebrations they shared a meal which spanned many nations. Everyone brought food traditional to their country. Some dishes were home-made, some were takeaways. The feeling of companionship and togetherness was strong.

Memorial

Ben's friends made an entry of his details and dates on the internet on The Virtual Memorial Garden site.

Reflections

Ben's passing would be remembered for the way in which he had planned an imaginative send off in which everyone felt included. The tapestry of ideas contributed by his friends added to the richness of the occasion.

Notes:

- National Aids Helpline: 0800 567 123.
- Canal boat coffin and other special designs from Vic Fern. Tel: 0115 927 1907.
- The service was written and conducted by Interfaith Minister Rev. Jacqueline Clark.
- The Association of Interfaith Ministers and Spiritual Counsellors. Tel: 01643 862621.
  Email: halsecombe@aol.com
  www.interfaithministers.org.uk

FLYING HIGH

The elderly gentleman's wishes to be buried on the farm he had loved so much were fulfilled by his family. Conducted by a Minister from a Free Church, the service included the burial and was followed by a family picnic, kite-flying and the planting of acorns.

Introduction   Longwood Farm had belonged to Ned's family for generations. As he became increasingly debilitated he asked his son Giles to make enquiries regarding farm burials for him and his wife May for when the time came. Giles telephoned the Natural Death Centre, which sent a copy of its handbook containing a wealth of useful information which enabled him to carry out his father's wishes with ease; he was surprised at the lack of complexity regarding burial on private land. (See Appendix Two). The close family agreed to organise the funeral themselves without the aid of a funeral director.

After a long and fulfilling life, Ned fell into a deep sleep at home; the last thing he would have heard was the sound of familiar voices laughing and chatting which made him feel contented—not hushed whispers.

Arrangements

Ned was to be kept at home. Following the Doctor's visit the District Nurse came to wash, clothe and lay out his body. She suggested hiring an air conditioning unit as the weather was warm for September. Giles, meanwhile, dug the grave, using a mechanical digger, shoring up the sides and covering the hole with timber for safety.

Ned had always been respectful of all religions, and the Minister from the Unitarian Church came to discuss the content of the service with the family, which would appropriately be based on the harvest.

A personal and meaningful celebration that reflected Ned's life and beliefs emerged. Everyone was invited to bring a picnic to share and a kite to fly after the burial. The occasion offered a natural opportunity for a gathering.

Coffin

A simple pine coffin was ordered by mail order with 36-hour delivery which Giles lined with hay from the fields. Ned lay in his favourite clothes with his dog keeping vigil at his side. The front parlour was lit with candles as in past times; friends came to visit Ned, the children being given a choice as to whether they wished to be included. Ned's great granddaughter popped a favourite teddy beside the old man.

Flowers

Everyone collected autumn flowers from their own gardens—michelmas daisies, dahlias, berries and autumn leaves, which created a splash of seasonal colour.

<u>Transport</u>	The older children helped to groom and make ready the old horse and hay cart on which Ned would be transported to his place of rest.
<u>Location</u>	Before crossing the threshold of Longwood Farm for the last time, the Minister said a short prayer for Ned and his family. Everyone gathered in the yard as the coffin was secured on the straw-lined cart and surrounded with a tangle of freshly picked autumn splendour. Eyes misted with emotion as the procession assembled; it was like a scene from a nursery rhyme, proceeding up the winding track led by several excited dogs, the minister, then the horse and cart led by Giles.

Cows peered inquisitively over the hedgerow as the procession passed. The place chosen for the burial was in rolling pasture, which looked down towards the farmhouse with breathtaking views beyond. Instead of bare earth, hay was scattered into the void that now resembled a cosy nest.

<u>Service/</u>
<u>Ceremony</u>

Everybody gathered around the grave as the minister read the words by Edith Sitwell: "Love is not changed by Death, and nothing is lost and all in the end is harvest."

- Ned's love of the countryside was reflected in the prayers that followed.
- His grandson played 'We Plough the Fields and Scatter' on his flute.
- Giles spoke about his father's life, likening it to the cycles of nature.
- Ned's body was to become part of nature, which for him was just as it should be. The flowers were piled high as the coffin was gently lowered into the grave with the aid of ropes; the Minister

read an extract from 'Instructions' by Arnold Crompton.

- The family had requested especially that the traditional words "Earth to earth, ashes to ashes, dust to dust" not be used.
- The service ended with a reading of 'Do Not Stand at My Grave and Weep':

> Do not stand at my grave and weep;
> I am not there. I do not sleep.
> I am a thousand winds that blow.
> I am the diamond glints on snow.
> I am the sunlight on ripened grain.
> I am the gentle autumn rain.
> When you awaken in the morning's hush,
> I am the swift uplifting rush
> of quiet birds in circled flight.
> I am the soft stars that shine at night.
> Do not stand at my grave and cry;
> I am not there. I did not die.

> *Anonymous*

A copy of the poem was available for everyone to take with them. The grave would be filled in after the party.

Refreshments   Rugs were laid on the grass and young and old alike tucked heartily into the picnic. Eyes focused upwards as the children flew kites—like free spirits.

Memorial   Before leaving, the youngsters planted acorns; the oaks would hopefully survive the years, becoming memorials to Ned. His grandson selected a special stone from his collection, which he placed on his grandfather's grave. The children all piled onto the hay cart for the return journey down the track back to Longwood Farm.

Reflections

It was agreed by all that the act of creating the occasion had been a healing experience. May asked Giles emotionally, "Will you do the same for me when my time comes? It was all so beautiful!"

Notes:

The farm now belonged to Giles. The day had given him an idea: if farming became much more soul-destroying, diversification to become a Green burial ground may be the solution to survival. Planning permission would be required for the changed use of land.

- Natural Death Centre. Tel: 0871 288 2098.
- For information regarding burial on private land see Appendix Two.
- Mail order coffins.
  Vic Fern & Co Ltd., Nottingham.
  Tel: 01159 771571.
  Vic Fern & Co Ltd., Isle of Wight.
  Tel: 01983 531734.
- With the money saved by arranging Ned's funeral themselves, the family donated a generous amount to the charity 'Send a Cow'. Farmyard animals are purchased and given to poor families in Africa, aiding their survival and independence. Tel: 01225 447041; www.sendacow.org.uk

SACRED CIRCLE

A peaceful, spiritual atmosphere prevailed as Lisa's body was laid to rest in an orchard grave. Friends organised the funeral and conducted the ceremony, which included a candle meditation, circle-dancing and a shared vegetarian meal with champagne.

Introduction

Lisa had worked in a general practice where both medical and complementary medicines were combined. When she became terminally ill, Lisa's sister Jill came to look after her. Therapist friends gave Lisa treatments, which soothed and relaxed her, helping Jill in the ways they could.

Anxious to be allowed to die at home with the people she knew and trusted, Lisa moved to a downstairs room where she lay listening to music—which connected her to her own inner wisdom—while candles burned continuously.

The Healthcare Plan, which she followed closely, treated her condition with natural care using complementary remedies where possible, including flower essences from around the world.

Following Lisa's death the GP issued the death certificate. Having been washed in essential oils, Lisa's body was laid out, remaining in the cool room with no heating and the windows open. Scented candles, crystals and flowers surrounded her body until the final arrangements for the funeral were complete. She lay undisturbed in the cool airy room for three days, allowing her spirit to release itself from her physical body.

Arrangements

Lisa's group of like-minded friends frequently talked about life and death, making a pact to support one another practically and spiritually, come what may.

Lisa had discussed with those close to her ideas for her funeral, which she knew was coming sooner rather than later. Together they designed a beautiful spiritual ceremony that honoured her independent free spirit. A promise was made to Lisa by her friends that they would carry out all the arrangements themselves.

The place of tranquillity and peace Lisa chose for her burial was an orchard belonging to friends. With their permission and following the guidelines (see Appendix Two), the arrangements were soon complete.

Coffin

On the day of the funeral friends came to say goodbye to Lisa as she lay in an ethereal, blue wrap, into the pockets of which messages of love were secreted. Lisa hated coffins, so her body was placed on a biodegradable hessian burial stretcher, covered with a shroud and a drape.

Flowers

The language of flowers was closely adhered to; single blooms were selected by her friends which would become a part of the sacred ceremony.

Transport

A friend's Renault Five with the passenger seats removed was used to transport Lisa's body.

Location

Wind chimes and tiny lanterns hung amongst the gnarled branches of the glorious old apple trees in the orchard. A garden awning had been erected beside the grave, which offered mourners shelter from the drizzle and was where the ceremony took place.

An altar had been created on which candles and essential oils burned—sandalwood and juniper, where crystals of high vibration were placed: herkerken, donbite, kwizite and the stripy, almost transparent flounté.

Service/ Ceremony

Everyone gathered as the stretcher bearing Lisa's body was carried by friends and placed on a prettily clothed table beneath the awning. Flower heads were scattered to form a sacred circle about the body, around which everyone stood holding hands.

- The circle created a focus for their thoughts as they joined in a short prayer, which was led by Lisa's sister.
- The candle on the altar was the main flame from which everyone lit smaller candles. This ritual provided a strong energy within the circle.
- Prayers followed, inviting Lisa's soul to become one with the universal spirit and to be reunited with loved ones and with nature.
- They stood quietly, in turn recalling memories, speaking straight from the heart.

- The grave was blessed before the stretcher-bearers, using ropes threaded through the handles, gently lowered the stretcher bearing Lisa's body into her resting-place.
- The flower heads were tossed into the grave as friends said her name.
- Prayers of love and healing followed.
- A friend with a guitar played and sang a song, which reflected Lisa's life.
- They all held hands, moving clockwise, not as planned around the grave as it was raining too hard, but beneath the nearby awning. Moving slowly in a circle they danced the 'Angel Dance'.
- The 'singing bowl' was struck with a small wooden mallet; it sang with the sound of the creation of the universe—invoking the sacred. "Om" was chanted three times and followed with a silent meditation.
- Moving back to the graveside, they took turns with the shovel, replacing the soil. Before leaving they lit the lanterns which hung in the trees surrounding the grave.

Refreshments A champagne picnic at the graveside had been planned but the weather was too inclement. Instead, a shared vegetarian meal which included many hot dishes, had been prepared and enjoyed in the warmth and comfort of a friend's home. They drank a champagne toast to Lisa and to the circle of life.

Memorial A rustic cross marked Lisa's resting place and the seeds of flowers with healing properties were scattered on the grave and around the orchard.

Reflections A feeling of warmth and achievement was shared by all Lisa's friends at having fulfilled her wishes to be laid to rest in peace and solitude. Burial on private land had proved to be much simpler than they had imagined.

If the orchard were to be sold one day, the friends would still have their treasured memories.

Notes:

- *The Natural Death Handbook.* Tel: 0871 288 2098.
- For information regarding burial on private land see Appendix Two.
- The Jerrards Bio-Field stretcher and shroud. Tel: 08707 304050.
- Flower essence combinations, including emergency ones and tissues, were on hand throughout the day should there be a need.
- The music in which Lisa found such comfort was 'Graceful Passages' on CD with an accompanying book containing words of solace.
- Two books written by Andrew Tressidder, a GP of the new generation of doctors such as the one with whom Lisa worked, are: *Lazy Persons Guide to Emotional Healing* and *I'm Fine!—Learning to Unblock Your Emotions.* Both published by Newleaf.

LAST ORDERS

A service arranged by family and friends soon after Christmas, Tim took his final journey to the crematorium in a bright red coffin. A festive mulled wine and mince pie reception followed. His ashes were later dispersed in seven very different ways.

Introduction

When Tim and Kath married, between them they had five children under the age of eight years! Being step-parents had not always been easy; it had been Tim's humour that had kept them all going. Shortly before his death he had been amused by the film 'Last Orders' in which the deceased's ashes were taken by friends on a trip down memory lane before being scattered from Margate Pier. He found the idea of bizarre send-offs entertaining, and his own last order was realised with humour and thought.

Arrangements　　When the time came Kath was not in a position to think rationally or make suggestions. She was grateful that they had discussed their arrangements and taken out pre-paid funeral plans several years earlier.

Tim's death came at a particularly difficult time, just prior to Christmas. The Funeral Directors took responsibility for all necessary arrangements until the holiday passed.

The family had grim memories of impersonal conveyor belt funeral services at the crematorium bearing no resemblance to the individual's life. Backed by some friends, they decided to create their own special service and music for Tim. Thus everyone was involved in whichever way they felt comfortable.

Coffin　　Prior to his death, Tim had ordered a new car in a vibrant shade of red, and although a traditional coffin had been part of the agreed package, the Funeral Directors obliged by supplying a bright red coffin to take him on his final journey.

Flowers　　The floral tribute from Kath was an enormous spray of flowers in red and yellow which, on the red coffin, reflected the warmth of the season.

Transport　　Both the hearse and stretch limousine in which the family chose to travel drove past a spectacular feature fronting on to the crematorium. A large cross had been marked out on the grass, following Christmas, and was now filled with holly wreaths—tributes to loved ones and a treat for hungry birds.

Location　　A double slot had been booked at the crematorium, which avoided the feeling of being rushed. Kath had previously removed the artificial flower arrangements, replacing them with red poinsettias.

<u>**Service/**</u> <u>**Ceremony**</u>	The service sheets had a scanned image of Tim enjoying a family holiday on the cover; the proceedings focussed on the celebration of his life.

- Tim's daughter welcomed mourners, explaining why the family had chosen to organise the occasion themselves.
- Proceedings were interspersed with Kath's son playing his guitar and singing 'The Long and Winding Road' by the Beatles and 'Not Fade Away' by the Rolling Stones.
- A letter from an elderly friend, who through ill health was unable to attend, was read aloud.
- Many humorous memories of Tim were recalled by members of the family.
- A short silence gave mourners the opportunity to say goodbye to Tim in their own personal way.
- Kath led the mourners in The Lord's Prayer.
- Tim's eldest son pressed the cremator button himself.
- Everyone was invited to join the family for refreshments.
- Finally, Elton John's 'Candle in the Wind' was played as everyone took leave of the chapel.

The floral tributes were displayed, each bearing an enclosure card with a message; later these were collected by the funeral director and returned to Kath.

<u>**Refreshments**</u>	Hot mulled wine and mince pies were served in a hall near their home. CD's of Tim's favourite classics played in the background as everyone exchanged memories and reminisced over photographs.
<u>**Memorial**</u>	Tim had read a newspaper article about little clay pots that were made to hold a small amount of ashes. The idea had captured his imagination. As they had

agreed, Kath ordered one each for herself and their children, enabling them all to remember Tim's life in their own way according to their varying ideas and beliefs. Kath would keep her pot of ashes to be scattered with her own.

Summary of the article Tim read by Gemma-Nesbit: While travelling on a bus in India Gemma sat next to an elderly woman who carried a huge knapsack on her back. When asked by Gemma what she carried, she replied, "My husband". There were many small clay ash pots, a tablespoon of his ashes in each. She was travelling the world, dropping one into the Ganges, Thames, Indian Ocean and so on.

Reflections

Christmas had been an emotional time and the waiting difficult, but it had given everyone time to reflect and prepare for Tim's farewell. Following their initial panic they realised that as long as the body was in safe keeping there was no rush to finalise the arrangements.

Notes:

- Extra costs were involved beyond the pre-paid package, e.g. an extra slot at the crematorium, containers for ashes and the red coffin.
- Ash Pots by Gemma Nesbit. Tel: 01308 485211

HOLE IN ONE

Following Jack's sudden death on the golf course his funeral arrangements echoed his passion for the game. A service at the crematorium was followed by an imaginatively themed buffet lunch at the club. His ashes were scattered on the golf course at a later date.

<u>Introduction</u>   Jack had recently retired, thus enabling him to take up some serious golf. He always felt happy in the wind and rain, if not playing, then walking his dog, observing nature, the seasons, animals, flowers and birds. He had formed an in-depth interest in insects while searching for lost balls in the rough.

It was a shock to everyone when he suffered a fatal heart attack on the course. As Jack's death was unexpected, a post-mortem had to be carried out.

Arrangements

The subject of death had been little spoken of within the family, and Jack's widow Liz, and daughter Jenny, were inconsolable. They received great support from a firm of funeral directors, which guided them through the formalities. Liz was in a dilemma; she felt that in order to express her love she should choose the most expensive funeral. Not being accustomed to dealing with finance she felt confused and worried but did not wish to appear mean. The Funeral Director was flexible and responsive to her concerns by offering a detailed estimate in advance.

Jack had no religious beliefs and it seemed hypocritical to have a minister take the service, but Liz knew of no alternative. It removed an enormous burden from her when the Funeral Director suggested contacting an officiant from The British Humanist Society who would personally write a service the family could all feel happy with.

The Officiant visited their home earlier in the week; they talked about Jack's life and together designed a simple ceremony of quiet dignity that gave those present an opportunity to pay tribute to a kind and gentle man.

Coffin

It was decided that Jack should be laid to rest in his favourite golfing attire and that a score card indicating a 'hole in one' should accompany him.

Flowers

The wreath from his golfing friends had golf balls worked in amongst the flowers.

<u>Transport</u>	It had been suggested that the hearse take a short detour on the way to the crematorium, taking Jack past his beloved golf course for the last time.
<u>Location</u>	Everybody gathered outside the crematorium in the autumn sunshine as Jack arrived in the reassuring hands of the Funeral Directors.

Being a Humanist ceremony, the cross on the altar had been removed and the space filled with flowers; the hymn books had also been taken away for the duration of the service.

<u>Ceremony</u>

- The Officiant introduced herself and explained the reasons that Liz had chosen a non-religious Humanist service.
- A golfing partner of Jack's read a poem.
- A colleague gave a tribute.
- Mourners stood for the committal as the curtains drew around the coffin.
- A short silence for private thought then took place.
- Finally, the Officiant issued an invitation on behalf of Liz and Jenny to join them for lunch at the golf club.
- A CD of the Floral Dance played while mourners left the chapel.

<u>Refreshments</u>

The club stewards provided an imaginative themed finger buffet with everything flagged accordingly:

- A selection of 'sand wedges'
- Pro Specials
- Niblets
- Birdie nibbles
- Hookers
- Hole in one

- Toppers
- Junior eagles
- Chippers

Everyone bought their own drinks from the bar.

Memorial

By arrangement with the Golf Club Manager, Jack's ashes were scattered on the course at a later date and Liz had a wooden bench placed near the 18th hole for all who wished to sit, rest and remember.

Reflections

Liz resolved to make a will and finalise her own funeral arrangements, discussing them openly with her daughter before the time came, thus relieving Jenny of some of the burden they had experienced following Jack's death.

Notes:

- Liz felt well supported on the day of the funeral, but the shock of her husband's death left her feeling isolated and lonely. Everyone seemed to shun her, even crossing the road to avoid conversation. She so longed to talk to someone about Jack. Eventually her doctor recommended that she join a bereavement group where she found great solace. Tel: British Association for Counselling (BAC). Tel: 01788 550899 bac@bac.co.uk.

- The ceremony was written and conducted by a celebrant from The British Humanist Association. Tel: 020 7430 0908; www.humanism.org.uk

CELEBRATION OF A CENTURY

Vi was in her 109th year when she died. Her life, which had spanned from Queen Victoria's reign until after the Millennium festivities, was celebrated in a service which included many of her unique memories.

Introduction

Miss Violet Slarke was one of the few people who could genuinely claim to have lived in three centuries. She slipped peacefully away at the rest home where each day she had lived with a sense of purpose.

It has been an honour for me to have known this wonderful lady who shared her historical memories with me; especially those of Queen Victoria's funeral which she had witnessed while waiting with her parents in the Long Walk at Windsor as a three year old.

When the horse-drawn gun-carriage passed bearing Queen Victoria's coffin, the procession was on its way to the mausoleum at Frogmore, near Windsor, where the Queen's body was to be laid beside that of Prince Albert, her consort.

Vi was wearing a red riding hood cape made by her mother with the addition of a black arm band—she remembers with embarrassment sticking out like a 'sore thumb'! Everyone around her was dressed in deep mourning—black. The men doffed their hats as the sombre procession passed.

Vi's Funeral

Many years later, as I stood beside Vi's coffin at the crematorium, I wondered if she was wearing the beautifully tailored silk suit that she had stitched by hand for her 108th birthday party at which she had played 'Happy Birthday' to herself and her guests on the piano.

Flowers

An exquisite spray of sweet scented lilies lay on Vi's coffin from her many nieces and nephews.

Service

The Vicar delivered a powerful service of celebration which, included:

- A warm welcome to all those present.
- Vi's great-nephew read a poem written by her at the age of 107 which had recently been published.
- Loving letters from great-nieces in Australia (both school teachers) were read aloud by the Vicar. Having been a schoolmistress herself, Vi corresponded enthusiastically in beautiful handwriting

with schoolchildren in many countries. She enjoyed hearing their modern news as they in turn savoured her historical knowledge.

- Everyone stood for the committal. "To everything there is a season and a time to every purpose on earth, a time to be born and a time to die"— Ecclesiastes 3:1-8.

Memorial

At her request Vi's ashes were interred in the family grave at Towcester where she had lived and taught and where she could rest in peace alongside her mother, grandparents and others so dear to her. The graveside service was attended by relatives and friends, who laid posies of garden flowers on her grave. It was the town where she had waved to the soldiers returning from the Boer War and had played tag, skipping and hopscotch in the lanes, occasionally dodging a horse and cart. It was here that she saw a motor car for the first time, parked outside the sweet shop where she could buy liquorice sticks or sugar mice for a farthing.

Author's Note

I have many wonderful handwritten letters from Vi; also, a beautifully embroidered and beaded velvet box made by her at a craft class just weeks before her death.

FRED'S LEAVING PARTY

A pre-planned celebration of life for a spiritualist and a service at the crematorium which included party dress and musical nostalgia.

Introduction Fred's illness had allowed him time to tidy his affairs and plan his funeral the way he wanted it to be. Affirming the continuity of life after death enabled him to make the arrangements in a light-hearted way without fear. As a medium himself, Fred had helped many bereaved persons on the road to recovery following their grief or loss. A friend from Fred's church gave him healing on a regular basis, which was relaxing and would help him with a peaceful transition when the time came.

Arrangements

Having confirmed the arrangements with a local funeral director, his son Jim and the church minister, Fred admitted to a sense of relief but added that he was not ready to "turn up his toes just yet".

An announcement at the Spiritualist Church the Sunday following Fred's death invited friends to his 'leaving party'. He had requested that everybody wear party attire, threatening to come back and haunt anyone daring to wear black!

Coffin

Fred chose an economical coffin, considering it to be simply a container for his remains, knowing that only his body had died and that his spirit would live on.

Flowers

Fred's favourite hat and stick were placed on the coffin along with a brightly coloured spray of flowers from his family, and a union jack worked in red, white and blue flower-heads from the British Legion acknowledging his war work. Donations made in lieu of flowers were sent to the Royal National Lifeboat Institute, since Fred had been a crewmember as a young man.

Transport

The local firm of Funeral Directors dealt with all formalities including the transport.

Location

As everyone gathered outside the crematorium, bags of fruit drops were handed around. This had been Fred's Sunday tradition, but on this occasion it was the turn of another to supply and hand round the 'sweeties'. Fred's coffin, covered by a beautiful handmade quilt, was in place as the mourners entered the chapel.

Service/ Ceremony

Following a warm welcome from the Minister everybody sang 'All Things Bright and Beautiful'. This wasn't easy with a mouthful of sweets, but it created the sort of uplifting occasion Fred had yearned for! The minister spoke of Fred's wonderful humour and his longing to be reunited with loved ones, including several pets. She also recalled the occasion on which he had made the arrangements for this day. Mourners stood as the curtain drew around the coffin, and the room filled with nostalgia as Vera Lynn's voice sang out 'We'll Meet Again'. Everyone left the crematorium with tears in their eyes—not only of sadness but with memories of a much loved man. The occasion was classified by all as a 'good send-off'.

Refreshments

Many people contributed food for the reception, which took place after the funeral at his son's home. A photograph of Fred as a young man wearing his army uniform stood beside a bowl of fragrant sweetpeas forming the table centrepiece.

Memorial

Fred's name and dates were entered in a book displayed at the crematorium, which would be available for viewing on every anniversary.

Jim collected his father's ashes from the funeral director and mailed them to the Royal National Lifeboat Institute office in the town where he had been a crewmember. It had been Fred's wish that his ashes be scattered in the sea off the rugged coastline he knew so well.

Reflections

Fred's funeral had only been tinged with sadness; he had relieved his family of making decisions and, as always—he did it his way!

Notes:

- The RNLI Tel: 01202 663000.
- When registering a death the following information is required:
  Date and place of death.
  Deceased's last (usual) address.

Deceased's first name, surname and maiden name, if appropriate.

Deceased's occupation and the occupation of his/her spouse (if applicable).

Whether the deceased was receiving a pension.

If the deceased was married, the date of birth of the surviving widow/widower.

A certificate of burial/cremation is then issued, allowing the funeral to take place.

Author's Note   Fred's Leaving Party was the first funeral I had attended where I was left with a feeling of exhilarated excitement which led me to write this book.

GREENFINGERS

Following an intimate family service in Ron and Betty's garden, the Vicar accompanied Ron's body to the crematorium for committal. His ashes were interred within a sundial that was eventually placed in the garden, forming a focal point at a memorial service held some weeks later.

<u>Introduction</u> Ron and Betty had celebrated their 50th wedding anniversary in the month of September, almost a year before Ron's sudden death. For their entire married life they had shared a love of gardening. Ron had often spoken of his wish to be buried in the garden that he loved so much. When the time came,

70

although it seemed an unlikely possibility, Ron's son contacted The Natural Death Centre that gave him the relevant information (see Appendix Two.) Although this was a possible option, Ron's son felt the idea was impractical, for if his mother wished to move she would have to leave her husband behind. Further, to have a body buried in the garden would almost certainly affect the price of the house.

Arrangements

As an alternative choice to garden burial the family arranged a short service led by the local Vicar, which was held in their garden.

As the funeral was limited to close family only, a memorial service was arranged on what would have been their 51st wedding anniversary. Invitations were sent out after the funeral, inviting everyone to the service, which was to be followed by lunch.

Coffin

The local Funeral Directors supplied a simple pine coffin with rope handles and, at Betty's request, Ron was dressed in his gardening clothes.

Flowers

A single wreath created with vegetables from the garden was placed on the coffin. Donations were made to the National Society for the Prevention of Cruelty to Children (NSPCC), a charity close to Ron's heart.

Location

The small family group gathered in the garden beneath the weeping willow tree where the coffin had been placed on a low table.

Service/ Ceremony

The Vicar led a simple service, which included readings and a favourite poem which Ron had remembered from childhood and had often recited. The service focused on the garden, which restored the spirit and lifted the soul.

Cremation

The family having said goodbye to Ron with love and dignity, the Funeral Directors carried the coffin to the waiting hearse. The Vicar accompanied Ron's body for the committal at the crematorium.

Refreshments   Light refreshments were served in the house.

Memorial Service   A month after the funeral, guests gathered for a short service of remembrance, during which the Vicar unveiled a sundial containing Ron's ashes in the centre of the lawn. This would be Betty's personal shrine, to remain with her wherever she went. The sundial, cast in bronze with an antique finish, allowed room for Betty's ashes to be added at a later date.

Refreshments   A buffet lunch was prepared by Betty and her friends and was served on the terrace. Guests looked at photographs, shared memories and played Ron's favourite music.

Reflections   Although Betty's life felt empty, she was comforted knowing that her husband's funeral had been so personal and had taken place in the garden that he had loved.

Notes:
- A relative unable to attend the funeral sent Betty a rose bush, which bore its own message in its name, 'Blessings'.
- NSPCC. Tel 020 7825 2505; www.nspcc.org.uk
- The sundial can be ordered from any reputable funeral director.

WATERBUGS AND DRAGONFLIES

A funeral for a little girl buried in tranquil parkland in a beautifully painted cardboard coffin. The non-religious ceremony was conducted by a Celebrant and included a special story for the children, who then blew bubbles heavenwards.

Introduction

Paramedics did everything possible following the accident. Sophie's short life had ended abruptly, shattering the family's hopes and dreams; the shock had numbed their emotions. Sophie's parents, Chris and Alex, were grateful for the support of friends who knew of a privately owned natural burial ground and offered to drive them to view it. The couple were moved by the beautiful parkland and surrounding mature oak woodland. This was the resting-place they chose for Sophie. Their other two children were included in all aspects of the arrangements and things were discussed openly with them. Chris and Alex believed their children's involvement would help with their grief.

Arrangements

The Funeral Directors assisted them by making many suitable and sensitive suggestions; they also recommended a celebrant. Alex preferred a woman to conduct the non-religious service. A mother herself, the Celebrant visited the family and was also introduced to 'Spot' the dog! At first it was hard for them to talk but she asked to see photos and soon all the family were chatting about their memories of Sophie. It was as if a great weight had been lifted and the tears could flow as much from joys remembered as in grief.

Coffin

A flat-pack cardboard coffin was chosen which the family took home to decorate, a project that proved to be a healing experience. Using brightly coloured acrylic paint, a beautiful garden full of flowers and sunshine was created. Butterflies carefully cut out from stiff paper were glued in lifelike forms amongst the flowers; the delicate little creatures had always fascinated Sophie.

Alex and Chris wrote a loving letter to their little daughter, which they placed beside her.

Flowers

A teddy bear composed of white chrysanthemums was the tribute Ben and Alice had chosen for their sister. Many flowers were sent by family, friends and colleagues as symbols of sympathy and remembrance. The children helped an attendant carry the flowers to the graveside; meanwhile Ben was in charge of Spot who, just for this special occasion, was allowed to accompany them.

<u>**Transport**</u>	Sophie's body was collected from the hospital by the Funeral Directors specialising in Green funerals, in a green vehicle. Staff were dressed in the same discreet colour uniforms, not sombre black.
<u>**Location**</u>	From Sophie's burial plot there was a clear view of the fenced deer park. Shetland ponies with their foals grazed in a nearby paddock, while a wide range of birds and wild animals enjoyed the freedom of the tranquil setting. Buzzards, woodpeckers, owls and bats were frequently spotted.
<u>**Service/ Ceremony**</u>	Everyone was greeted in the private lounge at the burial ground where coffee was served. The Celebrant, wearing a stole embroidered with butterflies, led the group to where Sophie's beautiful coffin and the floral tributes waited in the parkland.

The Celebrant welcomed the gathering:

- Everybody sat on the grass at the graveside while she read aloud the story of the *Waterbugs and Dragonflies* by Doris Stickney, explaining death in a delightfully simple way to the children.
- Prayers followed which were also taken from the book; these included prayers especially for the parents.
- Sophie's sister played a well-rehearsed piece of music on her recorder, during which time a staff member operated the coffin-lowering device; the children blew glistening bubbles that soared towards the heavens.
- The Celebrant completed the service with the following words: "There are no words or rituals that can take away your pain, but be reminded, Sophie will live on forever in your hearts and memories."

- It was suggested that when people were ready, refreshments were available in the reception lounge. A butterfly accompanied the group as they took a slow walk back through the parkland; from now on butterflies would be symbols of Sophie's spirit.

The grave was filled and the flowers rearranged, ready to be viewed after tea.

Refreshments   The caterers served a selection of imaginative finger food and welcome cups of tea.

Memorial   The plot was marked by a numbered plaque bearing Sophie's name and dates, as well as a short epitaph. A plan of the site was available to visitors. Wild flower seeds were scattered. Within the next season a tree native to the area would be planted.

The family planned to have a firework display at the graveside each year on Sophie's birthday—with no bangs so as to avoid frightening the animals.

Chris created a border in their garden that was planted with flowers that would attract butterflies and would be a constant reminder of Sophie.

Reflections   Not being aware of the existence of natural burial grounds, Alex and Chris appreciated their introduction to the non-commercial, ecologically friendly and economical burial site, so much more sympathetic, they felt, than a graveyard.

Notes:
- Chris and Alex joined a grief recovery programme where they met other grieving parents.
- The many drawings and letters received from other children meant a great deal to the family.

- Cardboard coffins are available from funeral directors; also from Celtic Casket Tel: 01283 521104.
- Following the ceremony, Alex and Chris were particularly touched by a card sent by the Celebrant, which simply read 'Just a gentle reminder that I am here for you, your family and friends'.
- The ceremony was written and conducted by a celebrant trained by Choice Farewells. Tel: 023 8086 1256; www.alternativecelebrations.co.uk

IN LOVING MEMORY

A social club for people with sight loss was started over forty years ago in loving memory of Effie Jane Ross (known as Jane Ross). This is a reflective funeral plan for a member who died several years ago, which takes into account the special needs of the mourners.

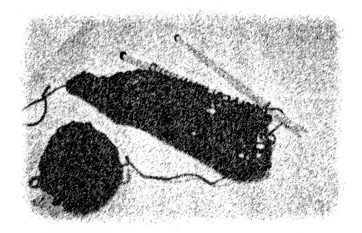

<u>Introduction</u>

The Jane Ross Club was started and named as a memorial to a special lady who throughout her life supported those with sight loss and in many cases physical challenges. The Club's social meetings began over forty years ago with sixty members; time has dwindled the numbers down to approximately twenty-five ageing members.

Blind from birth, Millie was one of the original members; she lived and worked within an institution then called 'School for the Blind'. Always cheerful, her excitement soared whenever Cliff Richard's voice was heard on the radio, which played non-stop in the handicrafts department where she spent her days. Millie was an example of courage and determination to all who knew her. I was unable to attend her funeral but the following is what I would have liked for her, had it been possible. The occasion is designed with the special needs of all her friends in mind.

Coffin

Throughout her life, Millie had only ever been aware of the colour black. Whether she was knitting, weaving or making a basket, working with bright colours gave her great pleasure. Whether it was sunshine yellow, sky blue or grass green, she thrived on colours she had never seen. In her fight for survival in a harsh and demanding world, I would choose for her the most luxurious coffin I am aware of—the 'White Silk' Ecopod. Her fragile body could rest peacefully upon the soft, sumptuous scarlet feather lining. Made from natural materials, the pod is overlaid with handmade mulberry silk and paper—beautiful in its simplicity, tactile and eco friendly.

A German tradition could be adopted by putting a piece of knotted string in Millie's coffin to avoid her being bored on the journey—she had after all shown enormous patience when untangling her knitting wool!

Flowers

Flowers of the brightest colours and sweetest perfumes would be an important part of the occasion.

Transport

With the avoidance of anything black, dark or depressing, a white hearse would be a most appropriate form of transport for Millie in which to take her final ride.

Location

Arrangements for the funeral would be discussed in detail with the crematorium manager, enabling able-bodied helpers to rearrange the chapel the evening before. Chairs would be set out in circles, leaving spaces for wheelchairs, and a prettily clothed table could be placed in the centre on which the coffin would be placed. The first two morning slots would be booked, ensuring mourners would not be rushed; this would also allow time to rearrange the chapel after the ceremony.

Service/ Ceremony

The service sheet would be produced both in large bold print and in braille. On the front cover words by Helen Keller:

The marvellous richness of human experience would lose something of rewarding joy if there were no limitations to overcome. The hilltop hour would not be half so wonderful if there were no dark valleys to traverse.

- 'I Can See Clearly Now' by Johnny Nash would be playing on CD as mourners take their places around Millie's coffin.

- The Minister would welcome the gathering to a celebration of Millie's life and to say goodbye. She would continue: "Although Millie was blind and so unable to see them, she delighted in colours that surrounded her. This wonderfully cheerful person we honour today by surrounding ourselves with brilliantly coloured flowers and by dressing in our brightest clothes. We rejoice that Millie has been released from her earthly limitations and can now experience her wholeness, safe in the arms of love. We treasure the memories of all that she has been in our lives and know that these will live on in our hearts forever."

- There could be a reading 'Flowers' from the litany of flowers in the Tibetan Book of the Dead.

- The Minister would speak of the cross Millie bore throughout her life, and bore with fortitude, inspiring many, including other members and helpers of the Jane Ross Club. Millie's love of the small things in life would be mentioned, especially her knitting. It didn't matter to her if some of the stitches dropped or if the wool became muddled. The end result was something unique. The Minister would continue: "Millie had a beauty of her own and today we are completing the casting off stitches of her earthly life."

- Everyone would hold hands and pray together.

- I would like to include the 'white stick ritual' and the Minister would go on to say: "Millie always used a white stick. It was an essential part of her life and she was never without it. Now she no longer needs it we have cut it up into small pieces and drilled a hole in the centre of each piece to make beads." Instead of the usual eulogy, several people who knew Millie and loved her would come and say a few words about her and thread one of these 'beads' onto a piece of string. The completed necklace would be given to the Jane Ross Club as a wonderful memento of Millie's life—each bead imbued with the memories of those who knew her.

- 'The Millennium Prayer' sung by Sir Cliff Richard (Millie's hero) would be played.
- Millie's coffin would be transferred from the table to the catafalque.
- Those able to, would stand for the committal, as the following words would be said by the Minister: "We let you go, Millie. Tonight there will be a new star shining in the heavens; never again will you be in darkness. May God bless you and keep you. Amen."
- Closing prayer.
- 'All Things Bright and Beautiful' would be played on CD as mourners make their exit.

Refreshments

A hall set with small tables and chairs with spaces for wheelchairs would be laid out prettily with bowls of fragrant flowers on each to please the senses. Selections of finger food, easy to eat, threaded onto wooden kebab skewers, would be served with long bendy straws available for those with restricted movement.

Reflection

The box containing Millie's remains would be collected from the crematorium and her life celebrated by scattering her ashes in the most beautiful, colourful and fragrant garden imaginable.

Notes:

- The ceremony was created by Interfaith Minister Rev. Jacqueline Clark. The Association of Interfaith Ministers and Spiritual Counsellors. Tel: 01643 862621. Email: halsecombe@aol.com www.interfaithministers.org.uk
- A white hearse may be hired through any reputable funeral director.
- An induction loop would ensure mourners' with hearing loss were able to participate in the service.
- ARKA Ecopod: 01273 746011; Email: hazel@ecopod.co.uk www.ecopod.co.uk

JOURNEY'S END

A railway theme built into the funeral arrangements for an autistic young man. Harry's cremated remains were interred at a scenic track-side burial ground, followed by a meal, which took place on the return train journey.

<u>Introduction</u>   When Harry died, mutterings of "what a blessed release" were overheard by his parents Vic and Lucy. They were devastated by their loss and extremely sad that some people were unaware of how much joy their gentle and affectionate son had brought into their lives. With learning difficulties, Harry had required constant support; the group of carers and young people with whom he had lived became his close friends and family. Vic and Lucy were anxious to celebrate their son's short life in a very special way, and the one thing that had always stirred his imagination had been railways. It seemed fitting, therefore, to incorporate this into his final journey.

Arrangements

Lucy and Vic proceeded to make arrangements for the cremation of Harry's body with the Funeral Directors who also recommended a celebrant trained by 'Choice Farewells'. The Celebrant visited the family home where, together with Lucy and Vic, he looked at photographs and talked about Harry's life, and began creating a special ceremony for a special person around his passion for trains.

Coffin

The Funeral Directors arranged for a hand-painted railway-theme coffin to be available.

Flowers

Flowers from the immediate family surrounded Harry's coffin. In many cases donations were made to the Autistic Society which had supported Harry throughout his life. It was a way in which friends could show their respect and offer comfort to the family at a time of such sorrow.

Transport

A hearse estate took Harry's coffin to the crematorium, where mourners were gathered.

Service/
Ceremony

Vic and Lucy chose the following words for the cover of the service sheet: 'In memory of our special son and for all the joy he brought into our lives.'

The Celebrant asked everyone to join the family in their sadness to say farewell to Harry, to remember and give thanks for his life.

- He continued by reminding those gathered how much Harry loved railways and explained that to commemorate that love, the chapel was to be looked upon as the platform of a railway station where Harry was to be seen off on his journey.
- Mourners joined with prayers.
- The Celebrant spoke of life being a journey where Harry was the engine; the coaches were those he had coupled up with and the passengers his family and friends he picked up and dropped off on his passage of life.
- Harry's uncle read a poem.
- The Celebrant continued: "As the train leaves our sight there are others awaiting the arrival at a heavenly station where Harry will once more be reunited by love."
- Everyone joined in saying the Lord's Prayer.
- The congregation stood as Harry's earthly remains were committed. The Celebrant blew the station-master's whistle as the curtain drew around the coffin.

Harry's ashes were later placed in an 'Arka Acorn Urn' which was left in the safekeeping of the funeral director until further arrangements were made.

Further
Arrangements

Having taken time to contemplate, it was decided that Harry's ashes should be interred during a ceremony which would continue the railway theme. A celebration of his 21st birthday would soon have taken place to which his friends and their carers would have been invited. Arrangements were made with their various special needs in mind.

Vic and Lucy contacted an independent, family-owned company that specialised in railway funerals, who helped plan the journey. A coach transported the Acorn urn containing Harry's ashes, the Celebrant and entire party to the Midland Railway.

On arrival at the centre everyone gathered in the Station Buffet for a cup of tea, while the young people were entertained by a working model railway display.

Memorial Service

The party made their way to the adjacent Victorian railwaymen's chapel where the Celebrant conducted a short service of remembrance.

- The Celebrant spoke about Harry's life, the journey he was on and blessed his ashes.
- Everyone joined in with prayers.
- The service ended on a light and positive note.

Carrying the Acorn Urn of ashes, the Celebrant led the party to the awaiting train where everyone climbed aboard. The guard waved his flag and blew his whistle as the engine responded and the journey began. The engine worked hard to pull the train up a gradient, through the narrow cutting towards Swanwick Junction. They steamed past the carriage and wagon repair yard and on past the country park, stopping at the railwayman's burial ground.

Interment

The interment of Harry's ashes took place at the scenic track-side cemetery. Everyone stood around the Acorn Urn in the tranquil setting while the Celebrant said a short prayer. As Harry's ashes were interred the engine gave a long, last blast on its whistle—just for

Harry. The Celebrant asked "that he may rest in God's own Pullman carriage and that his memory never be shunted into a siding and forgotten because he is stationed in the hearts of many people for ever."

The group re-boarded the train to continue their journey past the Golden Valley road bridge where the valley opens up to reveal a row of canal-side cottages and Jessop's monument.

At Ridings the guard tested the brakes, ready to start the return journey to Swanwick Junction.

Refreshments

Refreshments were served on the return journey while everybody sat at laid tables and tucked into 'The Station Master's Meal' which included soup of the day, steak pie, new potatoes, carrots and garden peas followed by 'pud'.

Reflections

Vic and Lucy felt pleased that Harry's friends, the people he had lived happily with for so long, had been able to share their son's final journey.

Notes:

- Ceremony written and created by a celebrant trained by Choice Farewells. Tel: 023 8086 1256; www.choiceceremonies.co.uk
- Peace Funerals, specialists in railway funerals. Tel: 08457 696 822; www.peacefunerals.co.uk
- The Arka Acorn Urn for ashes. Tel: 01273 746011. Email: hazel@ecopod.co.uk. www.ecopod.co.uk

MY DAD

These are my reflections on a production line cremation, which took place many years ago. With a lack of knowledge at the time, my way of making things special for 'My Dad' was to secrete tiny model creatures amongst the flowers and bake his favourite cakes.

Introduction   Dad's Divine was in nature rather than in formal religion. My stepmother Clare, being the daughter of a vicar, was brought up with strict Christian guidelines; she and Dad were however able to reach a satisfactory compromise. While Clare attended services or polished the church brasses, Dad would be tending his large and productive vegetable garden or growing flowers which were often used to decorate the church.

An overwhelming fear of having to live without my dear, kind and gentle Dad haunted my childhood. As he grew older he stated clearly that "when I can no longer pull up my own trousers, it will be time to give in"; when the day came, he did! As a grown woman I screamed and shouted hysterically but I realised in my heart that he knew best.

Next day, I received a card from a friend bearing the following words by Canon Henry Scott Holland, which gave me great comfort:

Death is Nothing

Death is nothing at all. I have only slipped away into the next room. I am I and you are you; whatever we were to each other, that we are still.

Call me by my old familiar name. Speak to me in the easy way you always used. Put no difference into your tone.

Wear no forced air of solemnity or sorrow.

Laugh as we always laughed at the little jokes we shared together. Play, smile, think of me, pray for me.

Let my name be ever the household word that it always was. Let it be spoken without effect, without the ghost of a shadow on it.

Life means all that it ever meant. It is the same as it ever was. There is absolutely unbroken continuity.

What is this death but a negligible accident?

Why should I be out of mind because I am out of sight?

I am but waiting for you, for an interval, somewhere very near, just around the corner.

All is well.

Arrangements

A calmness befell me as I tore Dad's long johns into rags. He and I worked and talked together as we had on so many previous occasions. The brass and furniture began to shine in preparation for the gathering, which was to take place after the cremation. The act of 'doing' made me feel better.

The funeral arrangements were traditional; I had no knowledge of there being any alternative choices in those days.

Flowers

An abundant arrangement of mixed flowers from the family was placed on his coffin. The only thing I could think of to make it personal to him was to ask the florist to secrete tiny model ladybirds, dragonflies, butterflies and bumblebees amongst the flowers.

Looking back, I regret he didn't have his pipe, baccy and flat tweed cap with him. Having had a deprived childhood himself, he always supported Dr Barnados; donations in his name were made to this charity and to the Royal Society for the Prevention of Cruelty to Animals (RSPCA).

Refreshments

Following a short and impersonal service at the crematorium, of which I can remember little, everyone came home for refreshments. The days before had been spent in therapy—arranging flowers and baking all his favourites. As a youngster I loved baking him cakes and, however badly they had turned out, he ate them with relish, always offering compliments and encouragement.

Following his death a book fell at my feet in the library; the title was *Life in Spirit* written by the healer Harry Edwards. From this book I gained a great deal of knowledge and comfort.

Some months after the funeral I suffered a life shattering experience: the same evening I discovered Dad's framed photograph in pieces on the floor. This occurrence made me realise he was still around and able to comfort me with his presence at a time of real need.

A considerable time had passed when a friend asked me if I would like to accompany her to a Spiritualist Church, and I went in trepidation of the unknown. A perfect description of 'My Dad' wearing his flat tweed cap, smoking his pipe and of his unusually marked dog was given to me by the Medium. I was told that dad was franticly waving a white handkerchief to draw attention to it and was insistent that it was mentioned. As he grew older and was unable to walk long distances, Dad hung his handkerchief on a hawthorn bush at the end of a woodland path returning to the stile on which he rested. The dog was trained to return and fetch the handkerchief, thus doubling the length of her walk. There was no way that anybody present could have known about his solitary dog walks in a distant county.

Losing my Dad and having such wonderful proof of life after death has opened my mind and led me to discover sources of consolation I would not otherwise have been aware of. The sadness within this ending was the beginning of my journey in search of my own free spirit.

Memorial   Among the many items that he made that I will always treasure is a magnificent doll's house; the intricate fretwork must have taken hundreds of hours of infinite patience and incredible skill to produce.

Dad trained Lucy, my beautiful Golden Retriever puppy for me in the latter weeks of his life, and when he died it was as if his soul lived on in her. Thirteen years later when she died it was to me like a double bereavement.

Reflections

If it were possible to turn back the pages I would arrange a woodland burial for Dad, where he would be surrounded by the creatures of nature that had always been his love—with nesting boxes to encourage the birds, where squirrels scamper, hedgehogs forage and bats fly.

Coffin

I would commission a special natural pine coffin for him, which would be delicately stencilled with oak leaves. Should this design be ordered in advance of need it can be fitted with removable shelves, stood on end and used as a cupboard until required!

Ceremony

With awareness of the need for ritual, a ceremony would be created by his family and friends to honour his life and mourn his death.

Standing beneath the beautiful beeches around the grave, his spirit amongst us, a sacred space would be evoked in the magical woodland setting. The sprinkling of water would take place to the four dimensions—earth, air, fire and water—the water having been collected from the pond which had been the hub of the village in which he had lived happily for so many years.

Words spoken by Dad's lifelong friend Ron would offer a glimpse of a wonderful father, grandfather, uncle and friend.

The ceremony would be intermingled with silences, allowing time for private thought and also providing an opportunity to listen to the natural birdsong.

With the stencilled coffin blending perfectly into the setting, we would sit together either on logs or on nature's mossy carpet, sharing our personal memories of him.

Everyone would write on a card a special message or memory, which would be put on the coffin as it was lowered into a bed of familiar wood shavings.

The following messages have been contributed by some of those who would have been present:

- From son Jim: 'Dad, I remember especially the time when as a young boy you and I planted a walnut in the garden. When we sat together beside it you said: "One day, son, we will pick the walnuts together." The tree still flourishes to this day.'

- From his daughter Ann: 'Amongst the many memories I have of you, Dad, are the skilful ways you created whatever was needed, usually out of very little. You built the bungalow in which we lived and made the furniture inside. You grew the food we ate and made the toys we played with. I remember Polly and Suzie, the make-believe friends you and I played with and your Sunday afternoon nap when I brushed your hair.'

- His Daughter-in-law Daphne: 'Dear Dad, I remember your green fingers, the way you nurtured delicate seedlings into prize-winning blooms and delicious edible crops. I also remember your lovingly trained and obedient dogs that reciprocated your friendship.'

- His Grandson Nick: 'Whenever I think of you, Grandad, I think of our walks in the countryside, together with your little dog Pip. As we walked you talked to me and taught me about the plants and animals. You gave me a love for nature, which has lived on till this day. You had a special trick on the walk: you'd drop your handkerchief and when we got back from the walk you'd say to Pip, "Where's dad's hankie"—and Pip would rush off retracing our steps to find it. I remember, too, spending many happy hours with you in your workshop watching you repair and make things. The smell of wood was just like my idea of a proper workshop. You were a true craftsman and a real perfectionist.'

- His Granddaughter Carrie: 'To my Grandad. Thank you for passing on to me your passion for the countryside, the birds, the bees and all the animals; in fact, I hope I can continue your loving work here on earth. I am so sorry you are leaving us. The only good thing is that now I know that all the animals which pass over will be joining you. I can picture it now, you walking through heavenly meadows with our family dogs: Pippy, Dusky, Tinker, Lucy, Shelly and Susie. See you sometime, Grandad. Love and kisses, Caroline.'

- From Joan his niece: 'Uncle Tom [Mum's twin brother], you always made me laugh and brought fun into my life. I could tell you my troubles and you always listened. You called me "the little girl with the long pig tail." I shall miss you.'

- Ron's Daughter Joanie: 'I will always remember the wonderful family occasions we shared, especially the sunshine breakfast. Also, your little dog Pippy who always fetched your pipe and baccy. With my love, Uncle Tom—Joanie.'

- An old wind-up gramophone would then play a selection of Dad's favourite 78 records, including 'Trees' by Paul Robeson—a song he loved to sing.

- Dad could recite the poem 'Haiwatha' by Longfellow in its entirety, having learned it as a schoolboy; this would also be included.
- Following the lowering of his coffin and dedication of the notes and flowers, everyone would take turns with the shovel, replacing the chalky earth, while saying 'good bye'.
- On the journey home we would pause to share a picnic at the highest point on the Downs. Biodegradable balloons would be released—releasing Dad's spirit.

Memorial

Following a recent visit to the remote village where he lived, I noticed that the stile on which he used to rest had fallen into decay. The perfect memorial to My Dad can be provided by The Stile Company: a stile which would replace the old one—hand carved with oak leaves and wild flowers with a unique galvanised dog latch which he would appreciate and an inscription with the words 'In loving memory of Tom Morgan and his dog Pippy'.

Notes:

- Dad's name and dates are in the book of remembrance and his ashes scattered in the rose garden at the crematorium.
- The Stile Company—commemorative features in the countryside: Tel: 01295 780372; www.the-stile.co.uk
- Always with an eye to practicality he suggested that I had his ashes made into an egg timer when he was dead and gone. He never was one to be idle!
- Dad's lifelong friend Ron and father of my dear friend Joanie agreed that when one of them died, the survivor would become Dad to us both. I very much appreciated sharing her dad for many years.

- Dr Barnados' Homes. Tel: 0870 0101181.
- RSPCA. Tel: 020 8550 8822.
- LdR Coffin Design. Tel: 01179 744000

LET'S NOT PRETEND

An actress puts her affairs in order; meanwhile her hand-painted coffin is used as a coffee table. Eventually, the day of her funeral dawns wet and stormy—a funeral director's occupational hazard! She makes a dramatic exit by tractor, sunflowers, cat and all.

Introduction

Nesta decided to pre-plan her funeral for when, as she chose to put it, she 'kicked the bucket'. She reviewed her ideas from time to time, as she became increasingly aware of the many choices available to her and re-wrote the letter containing her wishes as her ideas developed.

Being rather eccentric and an actress her arrangements contained a touch of rebelliousness which suited her character perfectly. She discussed the practical arrangements with a Funeral Director who warned her about potential problems with access to the country church—her chosen venue in winter. Nesta kept a copy of her current letter lodged with her Solicitor; her daughter Amy was also aware of her mother's wishes and the whereabouts of the relevant documents.

Arrangements

Nesta's death took everyone by surprise; she was on tour many miles from home when the family received the news.

The Funeral Directors, with whom she had already spoken, collected her body and took over the arrangements according to her wishes.

Coffin

Conversation was never lacking in Nesta's home. Some time before her death she had commissioned an artist to paint happy, yellow sunflowers on her wooden burial box; wooden bun feet were also added, enabling her to use it in the meanwhile as a coffee table.

There were many unanswered questions Amy regretted not having asked her mother before she died. She wrote a letter containing those queries, putting it in the coffin beside her mother's body, hoping that one day Nesta would return through a medium with the answers.

Flowers

A dramatic spray of yellow sunflowers with cascading yellow and black ribbons lay on top of the burial box with the addition of a black cat whose glassy eyes looked on in defiance. Nobody had ever questioned whether the animal that had spent its life curled up on Nesta's bed had been a lifelike toy or a stuffed real cat.

Whichever, she had requested that it accompany her to the grave.

More large yellow sunflowers were used to decorate the church and Nesta's cottage—they had always been her favourite flowers.

Transport

Nesta's last drama was to be acted out by tractor and trailer to cope with the difficult access to the church in winter. The shoebox-shaped coffin (with bun feet removed) was secured to the trailer, which had to be towed across several acres of rough farmland to reach the church. The sunflowers and the cat travelled in the cab to avoid being blown away.

Location

The only other route to the tiny country church was through a woodland glade, across a rickety wooden bridge, then a climb up a muddy, slippery slope criss-crossed with gnarled tree roots. It had rained for days; large umbrellas were supplied by the funeral directors while mourners wore wellington boots and dressed suitably for the weather. Bedraggled sheep roamed in the churchyard, which was also a natural haven for birds, bees, butterflies and wild flowers.

Service/ Ceremony

Nesta's four sturdy grandsons, all of a similar height, carried their grandmother's coffin into church, where mourners were gathered. The building had been fitted with sound equipment for the occasion, songs from the shows and claps of thunder interspersed the Anglican service which included:

- Short readings from the Bible.
- Prayers and psalms.
- An old school friend of Nesta's gave the address.
- A reading from the New Testament, reminding the congregation of Christ's resurrection and promise of eternal life.

- 'Who wants to live for ever?' by Queen was the final piece of music to be played before everyone braved the elements and moved outside for the committal.

Burial

Nesta was to be buried in the family plot. A short service of committal took place as mourners stood shivering at the graveside, drawing closer together to hear the words recited by the minister: "Earth to earth, ashes to ashes, dust to dust"—words that were mingled with rumbles and claps of thunder. Her grandsons gently lowered Nesta's coffin into the grave—flowers, cat and all—using lowering cords. It was their last act of love to their grandmother. The printed service sheets had thoughtfully been enclosed in plastic to avoid rain damage.

Nesta's granddaughter obtained permission from the minister to video the occasion for the benefit of those who were unable to attend, including Nesta's fellow actors: the show had to go on regardless.

Refreshments

Some elderly mourners went straight to Nesta's cottage, being unable to make the slippery and hazardous journey to the church. When the others arrived back, cold and shivering, they were sitting comfortably beside a roaring log fire, drinks in hand.

Caterers served an interesting selection of hot finger food and steaming hot toddies to drive away the cold. Serviettes were printed with the faces of yellow sunflowers, thus carrying through the theme.

A video of the service and burial was played back during the reception to those unable to attend the service.

Memorial

Some time after Nesta's funeral, when the gravestone had been adjusted and her name and dates added, Amy planted a beautiful display of polyanthus on her mother's grave. She was reminded by the Minister that in compliance with public safety regulations no slug pellets should be used.

Reflections   Nesta's worldly exit had been even more dramatic than she could ever have anticipated. It had been her intention that the mourners should picnic in the churchyard as her Victorian ancestors had done after funerals. This idea had definitely not been an option but nevertheless the occasion had fully acknowledged the life of the lady that planned it.

Notes:

- With her will Nesta kept the following information:

letter of her wishes	passport
list of her investments	building society details
birth certificate	driving licence
marriage certificate	insurance policies
divorce certificate	bank details

- Primrose Hill: Supplier of hand-painted and eco-friendly burial boxes (pets or people). Tel: 07966 531229.

- Had Nesta wished to be cremated, her silicone implants would have had to be removed.

LIFE IS A CIRCLE

Alan had lived life to the full; his people-centred funeral was followed by the baptism and burial of his stillborn grandson. The handcrafted memorial, which was dedicated in a ceremony to Alan, had a tiny star included, which told of Wallie's brief existence.

<u>Introduction</u>   Alan, a Christian and a Spiritual healer, was diagnosed with incurable cancer. Becoming aware that he had only three months to live, he and his wife Judy and their 'spiritual family' of friends gathered; they shared thoughts and fears surrounding death openly over copious mugs of tea as they planned the funeral.

As Alan grew weaker, Judy notified their 'spiritual family' who in turn sat vigil some days and nights in the flickering candlelight, holding hands to give one another strength. At his passing a favourite meditation around swans, spoken by Judy, gave Alan great comfort, and as he died the wind chimes sounded as his spirit passed over.

At the moment of Alan's death the telephone rang. It was an old friend who had just had a dream telling her to contact him. Judy called the Doctor who issued the death certificate. The District Nurse came to wash and lay out Alan's body, wrapping him in a white linen sheet, placing a chain of rose petals around his neck and a bunch of white lilies at his side. Judy sat with their friends at his bedside, reading poetry and sharing stories all evening. Some were amusing, some were sad; they played beautiful music, amid laughter and tears. Bottles of wine were opened to celebrate living and dying, for Alan had lived his dying.

Arrangements

Jazz was playing on the stroke of midnight when, as had been arranged, the Funeral Directors collected Alan's body on a stretcher putting him into a shooting-brake.

Having said their goodbyes, the women took Judy into the garden to sit quietly in the balmy summer night, while the men tidied and made the bedroom pretty with flowers and clean sheets. One friend insisted on staying the night with her for company.

Coffin

Alan lay in his veneered ash coffin with some of his precious mementoes by his side.

Flowers

Alan's grandchildren did not attend the funeral but were represented by small posies of mixed flowers which were placed on the coffin.

Donations were made in Alan's name and sent to Marie Curie Cancer Care, which had provided the wonderful nurses who had helped look after Alan, enabling him to remain in his own home.

Transport

Accompanied by her family and friends, Judy walked to the chapel across the water meadows, a place where she and Alan had spent many happy hours watching the swans that featured in his favourite last meditation.

Location

A friend kept vigil as Alan's body lay in the candlelit chapel overnight. A sympathetic array of fresh flowers created a stunning effect as mourners made their way up the time worn steps into the ancient, cloistered building.

Service/ Ceremony

The hand-scripted service sheet bore details of the service. Being a Christian, Alan believed in the Christ Consciousness, love being the essence of his being, and of the gathering which celebrated his life. Contributions were made to the service by many friends including the Waynflete Singers.

- There was an introduction by the Minister
- The congregation then joined the singers in the hymn 'Dear Lord and Father of Mankind'.
- Readings by friends of Alan's came next:
    'Hope' by Emily Dickinson.
    'Heavenly Haven' by Gerard Manley Hopkins.
    'Do Not Go Gentle into that Good Night' by Dylan Thomas.
- Anthems were sung by the Singers:
    'Ave Verum Corpus' by Mozart.
    Stanford's 'The Blue Bird'.
    'Reflection' by William West.
- Amazing Grace was sung.

- Commendations followed.
- Copies of a poem written by Judy entitled 'Grief' were read silently during the service.
- Everybody then joined together to sing 'Jeruslaem'.
- Music was played, allowing time for private thought and prayer.
- An invitation to stay afterwards for refreshments was announced, both verbally and on the order of service sheet.

Burial

The Minister accompanied Judy and the family for a short service of committal at the cemetery. Judy and Alan had previously chosen and purchased a double plot where they had sat and spoken about their final separation.

Refreshments

Judy's sister organised refreshments for friends from the past and present and the many young people gathered in the village hall where, together, they enjoyed cream teas and chilled homemade lemonade. The family and the Minister joined the party following the burial.

Memorial Dedication Ceremony

One year later a unique gravestone commissioned by Judy was erected on Alan's grave. The occasion was celebrated with a dedication ceremony conducted by an Interfaith Minister.

- A friend sang Alan's favourite song and a professional musician played classical music on a violin.
- Each grandchild made a contribution to the occasion; the youngest scattered rose petals on the grave.
- A meditation also formed part of the ceremony.
- Finally they all held hands and danced around the grave.

The police were called by a passer-by who reported a suspicious ritual taking place in the cemetery!

Reflections

Despite her sadness Judy felt pleased that Alan had been able to die at home surrounded by the people he wanted to be there.

Being held by friends started Judy's healing process. Her only regret was that she didn't have a peal of bells for Alan; it would have been a way of rejoicing that he had lived, recognising that his death was just another stage of life and that he was now on a beautiful and sacred journey.

Shortly before Alan died his daughter-in-law shared with him her special secret—that she was expecting a baby. Some time elapsed before the sad news was revealed that the baby boy had been stillborn. The date of his death given by the hospital had been the same day that Alan had died.

The minister who had himself recently lost a grandchild under similar circumstances, empathised with the family and agreed to baptise the baby.

A short service took place at the funeral director's chapel, after which Wallie's little white coffin was taken and buried with Alan. A tiny star was added to the gravestone as a reminder of his brief existence.

Notes:

- Judy and Alan's spiritual family of friends were members of Psycho—Spiritual Initiative—a small network of people with a shared spiritual understanding offering, as a group, healing space for exploration, development and support. For further details telephone the following:

South/South East	Judy	01962 842853
	Marie	01962 862324
London	Christine	020 7622 4757

Midlands	Robert	0115 950 4336
North West	William	0161 881 5758
North East	Richard	07855 458634

- Stone mason Martin Cook; Cook Studios. Tel:01494 450828.
- Marie Curie Cancer Care. Tel: 020 7599 7777.
- Judy recommends planning your own funeral; when it's her turn she would like a similar, sensitive service with readings and anthems.
- The letters and cards received, many of which were from children, gave Judy great comfort.

A photo of the gravestone with its inscription added a final touch to the family album.

McCORMICK RECOVERY

Headed by a police escort, a procession of emergency vehicles, orange and blue lights flashing, followed the deceased's coffin on his son's breakdown truck to the crematorium. This unique mark of affection was shown for a well-respected man.

Introduction   John, his wife Val and sons Simon and Stephen, were all involved in the family business 'McCormick Recovery'. John rescued drivers and their broken down vehicles from all over the country and the continent. The heavier the vehicle and the more difficult the circumstances, the more readily he rose to the challenge. As a member of the Fire Service Preservation and the Solent Fire Engine Societies, John used his vintage vehicles to raise funds and give fun days out to youngsters suffering from cancer. He organised many local rallies and road runs, raising thousands of pounds for the Wessex Children's Cancer Trust. John's sudden death left an enormous void in the lives of many.

Arrangements

John had previously attended a funeral of a colleague who had been taken on a breakdown truck to his funeral. Simon and Stephen remembered that it had been their father's wish to have a similar send off.

Coffin

John's coffin was secured to the back of one of his own McCormick Recovery vehicles.

Flowers

A profusion of flowers in the company colours of red and yellow surrounded the coffin—the final tribute their friends could offer. Donations were also made in John's name to the Wessex Children's Cancer Trust.

Transport

It was a sight to behold, looking back at the never ending convoy of blue and orange lights flashing for miles behind the truck carrying John's coffin towards the crematorium. Led by a police escort, the cavalcade began from John's recovery yard. Friends came from all over the county to form the procession of dozens of vehicles, which included representatives from many of the major emergency services. They were joined by a number of vintage vehicles that included John's own rare fire engines.

Location

Firemen from Brockenhurst Fire Station stood in uniform, forming a guard of honour at the crematorium, an indication of the esteem in which John was held

Service/ Ceremony

The Minister led John's coffin towards the catafalque as the organist played one of his favourite hymns. The service focused on him being a forthright and outspoken man who was always willing to help others no matter how large or small the problem they had. Most of all he would always be remembered as a person who seemed to have a funny story to tell to match just about anything that could happen in life.

Refreshments Val's sister organised a welcoming reception after the service for all who were able to attend.

Memorial One of the many organisations in which he was involved was the local motor-cross club. Meetings were held in John's honour, and from that day onwards a John McCormick Memorial trophy was to be presented.

Reflections Feeling stunned by their sudden and unexpected loss, the family felt grateful to have been aware of John's funeral wishes; this gave them a starting point when making the arrangements.

Note: The family now treasures the condolences which were received in many forms—letters, poems, newspaper and magazine articles.

PROMOTED TO GLORY

*A medical student donates her body tissue to teaching and medical research.
A service of cremation followed a celebration of her life at the Salvation
Army Church. Annie's love of football was not forgotten, and her ashes were
sprinkled on the pitch.*

<u>Introduction</u>

Annie's diagnosis and prognosis were not good and it
took time for her to accept that she was very ill.
Having begun to train as a medical student in her
youth, and failed, she decided before her death to
donate her body to medical research. She discussed
her preference for body disposal with her next of kin

112

and was aware that legally they could overrule her wishes after death if they wished. She also informed her executors and GP of her intentions.

Arrangements

Taking the responsibility for her decision, Annie contacted Peterborough District Hospital which sent her an information pack and consent forms, that she completed and returned. The hospital in which Annie eventually died certified her death and issued a certificate, notifying Peterborough District Hospital which collected her body, returning it to her pre-arranged Funeral Directors within 24 hours. Her family made the arrangements as soon as possible with the guidance of a Salvation Army Officer who took into account Annie's requirements as a 'soldier'. The Funeral Directors posted notices in local and national newspapers with date, time and place of the funeral for the many other Salvationists who would wish to attend.

Annie's funeral service was to be a special occasion, which would celebrate all aspects of her life including her passion for football, especially the local team. She was affectionately known as 'Umbrella Annie'. Her distinctive blue brolly was proudly held aloft in every home game, often to chants of her name. In spite of her illness she never lost her passion for the sport.

Flowers

Two symbols of Annie's life lay on her coffin amongst the flowers—her old fashioned Salvationist's bonnet and the blue umbrella. Several large pedestals of blue and white flowers decorated the hall and were afterwards taken to the local hospital.

Coffin

Annie wore her Salvation Army uniform, of which she had always been proud, for this last journey. Being a soldier, her coffin was draped with the large yellow, red and blue flag of the Army.

Location

The congregation assembled in the Salvation Army Hall. Representatives from many organisations gathered with family, relatives and friends in an atmosphere of freedom and warmth—a hallmark of the Salvation Army. A white ribbon had been attached to the flag, indicating Annie's Promotion to Glory.

Service

The Army band played several pieces of spiritual music especially for Annie.

The service continued with:

- Congregational songs.
- Prayers.
- The reading of scriptures and a brief message.
- A tribute read by a friend.
- The singing group sang 'In the Sweet Bye and Bye'.
- A friend sang a moving solo expressing the life of Annie 'The Soldier'.
- A request to God was made that he comfort and bless the bereaved, helping them be faithful until death
- It was announced that refreshments were available and that anybody wishing to join members of Annie's family and the Minister would be welcome to do so for a short service of committal.

Cremation Service

Having celebrated the dedicated and serious side of Annie's life as a soldier, her family, who were not members of the Salvation Army, wished to acknowledge the fun loving Annie. A short but meaningful service at the crematorium took place.

Annie's coffin was carried into the chapel followed by the mourners in procession as the officer read the funeral service.

- The service began with prayers.
- A member of the football club spoke in a light-hearted way of Annie and how she would be missed as a supporter.
- As Annie's body was committed to the elements the curtain closed around the coffin and the Officer recited the benediction.
- To the surprise of a few, 'Football Crazy' on CD played as the mourners moved outside to where the floral tributes were displayed.

The funeral party soon returned to the Army Hall with its excellent facilities where a scrumptious spread was served including all Annie's favourites. The serviettes and flowers carried through the blue and white theme.

Memorial

- Some of Annie's ashes were scattered on the pitch of her local football team following a match, and a short silence was observed for a well loved character.
- Annie lives on in the hearts of many with a flowering cherry tree planted in her memory, a Chinese symbol of immortality under which the remainder of her ashes were scattered in the garden surrounding the Salvation Army Centre.

Reflection

Emotionally it had been a difficult time for the family but they felt pleased to have carried out Annie's wishes, and also to have added their own touches to the occasion.

Notes:

- The family revived a Victorian custom by placing a wreath of white flowers and ribbons on their front door.
- Peterborough District Hospital: 01733 874000.
  The hospital cannot guarantee to honour the deceased's wishes. A 100-mile radius for body collection, timing, presence of infection or coroner's involvement may put limitations on the agreement.
- The continuance of junk mail after Annie's death was the cause of great dismay to the family. They filled in a form and sent it Freepost asking that her name be removed from database and mailing lists. The Bereavement Register, Freepost SGA 1266, Sevenoaks, Kent, TN13 1SY.

SHALL WE DANCE

An elderly widower fills his lonely days with a study of environmental issues. His funeral reflects this interest and his love of dancing. The celebration of love conducted by an Interfaith Minister includes his wife's ashes.

Introduction

Sidney's wife Ada died only months after Sidney's retirement, leaving an enormous gap in his life. An interest in composting, recycling and environmental issues began to fill his long, lonely days. He read many facts that shocked him about emissions from crematoria where dangerous pollutants, carcinogenic dioxins, are released with each cremation, thus exacerbating global warming; a vast amount of domestic gas is used which horrified him. He read also that 10% of the mercury that is absorbed by fish in the North Sea comes from cremated people.

The eldest of his three children, Jane, did as much as she could to enable her father to maintain his own home for as long as possible and as he became more dependent other carers gave assistance.

Arrangements

Sid had spoken little of death, nor had he held any formal religious beliefs; Jane checked to see whether he had left any specific instructions before making arrangements. She followed the Age Concern fact sheet No. 27 'What to do when someone dies'. When organising the funeral Jane took into account the varying beliefs and religions of her brother and sister, who shunned the idea of mechanical funeral procedures.

With the assistance of an Interfaith Minister a unique ceremony was created for Dad who was to be reunited with Mum, the day he had waited so long for. Ada's ashes would become a part of the celebration, finally being interred with her husband.

Coffin

An eco-friendly pine coffin was chosen for Sid who wore his best suit and dancing shoes for the journey. Jane slipped a loving letter to her mum into his top pocket. Embalming would involve the use of eight pints of formaldehyde-based fluid, which would be pumped around Sid's body, subsequently being released into the ground. Their environmentally responsible dad would definitely not approve of this.

Flowers

A request for no flowers was made but any donations received would be made to Greenpeace, a group supporting Sid's ruling passion. Jane collected a selection of seasonal flowers, which were to be used in the ceremony.

Transport

Following their marriage, Sid and his new wife were loaned an Austin Seven for their honeymoon journey. After their many years of togetherness it seemed appropriate that they should make this last journey in style with no expense spared. A family decision was made to hire a 1931 Austin hearse which was heavily decorated with ornate ironmongery, and this grand old vehicle waited with Sid's coffin and the casket containing Ada's ashes outside what had been their retirement bungalow. Other vehicles joined the cortège, which was led by the funeral director who walked at a snail's pace, until reaching the end of the road.

Location

It was late autumn. The day was cold, but the hired hall with its modern facilities had been a good choice of venue in which to hold the ceremony. Chairs were arranged in circles around the coffin and casket, which were in place as mourners entered the candlelit space to celebrate the life of Sidney Thomas Black and to remember his wife Ada.

Service/ Ceremony

The Minister captured the old gentleman's uniqueness; she felt she had known him well, having shared his daughter's anxieties over the previous months. The celebration was one of pure love

'The Glory of Love' by Bette Midler was playing as mourners took their seats within the circle.

- The Minister introduced herself and welcomed those gathered to celebrate and honour the life of Sidney, to mark his release from the world and to feel joy in his reunion with his beloved wife, Ada.
- A reading 'Ascension' (from art card "You have a secret pair of wings") was then delivered.
- The Minister continued to explain the reasons for the choice of venue and that the ceremony was to mark Sidney's release from the physical world. The hall was chosen because it was a place of LIFE, a place to which Sidney came for his

Greenpeace meetings and where he and Ada had regularly taken part in tea dances. The family wanted this to be a joyous part of the ceremony, with Sidney present, followed by a social gathering. Later the family would attend the committal in the conservation area of the cemetery where Ada's ashes would be placed next to Sidney's coffin, symbolising their onward journey and acknowledging their undying love for each other.

- An invocation prayer was said.

- Jane read the eulogy. She spoke about her dad, remembering his loving, caring qualities as husband, father, grandfather and great grandfather. She recounted how difficult life was for him after the death of Ada and described how he had put all his energy into environmental issues. She spoke of her parents' undying love for one another, of their common love of dancing, and welcomed their reunion in spirit.

- The Minister continued: "Sidney and Ada loved dancing, they loved each other and they loved flowers. Their granddaughter will now read the beautiful poem 'Autumn' by David P Stuart."

- A reading came next.

- A basket filled with flowers and chocolates to share was passed around. The flowers were a reminder of the dance of life that Sidney and Ada wove together and the dance that they were now resuming; the chocolates were a reminder of the sweetness that is love, the love that never dies but lives forever in our hearts and minds.

- As the flowers and chocolates were handed around the music played: 'Could I have this Dance?' by Ann Murray.

- A few moments silence were observed for a healing meditation in which personal goodbyes to Sidney could be said; it was also a chance to give to Sidney's spirit any regrets, grievances or unfinished business that may still have lingered.
- The Minister then gave the blessing.
- On behalf of the family the Minister issued an invitation to everyone to stay on for refreshments and mentioned a surprise awaiting them outside.
- Everybody moved to a lawn beside the hall where four white doves waited in their cages. Sidney's great-grandchildren each released a bird: it was their special way of saying goodbye and we love you, Grandpa and Grandma.

Refreshments The music 'Shall We Dance?' by Anna from 'The King and I' was playing on CD as everyone tucked into the delicious spread organised by Jane's friend. There was plenty of chocolate cake—always a family favourite.

Venue The cemetery was designated as a conversation area, with the grass being mown once a year in October as if for hay, which was then collected and composted. Many wild flowers were evident and boxes had been erected in the trees to encourage the return of the owl population.

Burial Ada's ashes were placed in the grave with her husband. The immediate family and Sid's carers attended the brief burial conducted by the Minister; before leaving they tumbled handfuls of dry autumn leaves into the grave—it was like composting! Dad would have liked the idea.

Memorial Jane ordered some rose bushes and a bench for her garden in memory of her parents. Often she sat silently remembering; it was her own private way to grieve her loss.

Notes:

- The ceremony written and conducted by Interfaith Minister Rev. Jacqueline Clark. The Association of Interfaith Ministers and Spiritual Counsellors.
  Tel: 01643 862621
  Email: halsecombe@aol.com
  www.interfaithministers.org.uk

- Jane returned the borrowed medical equipment to the Red Cross.

- Hire of 1931 Austin hearse can be arranged through a reputable funeral director or direct from Cribbs. Tel: 020 7478 1855.

- The White Dove Company: Tel: 020 8508 1414; www.thewhitedovecompany.co.uk

- Donations were made to Greenpeace. Tel: 020 7865 8100; www.greenpeace.org.uk

- The service was recorded onto compact disc for the benefit of elderly relatives and friends who were unable to attend.

HIGH ROAD

A life lost, a life saved, following a road accident in the Highlands. The motorcycle hearse with Clergy Biker led the cavalcade of bikers to the crematorium. A roadside shrine and a stone cairn remain as marks of respect to a well loved young man.

Introduction   Having witnessed the fatal death of a friend, Scottish born Steve vowed always to carry an organ donor card. His father Scott being next of kin was aware of his son's intentions in case of an accident. While out biking with the lads, Steve was involved in a collision and pronounced dead shortly after arrival at hospital. His parents were given the bad news and asked to identify their son's body, and also to confirm their consent for organ donation. Scott and Jenny knew legally that they could override Steve's wishes if they wanted to but desired to honour their son's intentions.

Arrangements Steve's body was collected from the hospital by the Funeral Directors within twelve hours of the accident and was taken to their Chapel of Rest. Not having left a will, no executors had been nominated and therefore his parents made all the decisions.

Coffin Steve, who had been a keen footballer, was laid to rest wearing his red and white football attire in a coffin painted Firestone blue and silver, the colours of his bike.

Flowers A biker's boot worked in chrysanthemums with a heel spray of orange blooms was amongst the many floral tributes. Flowers also formed a roadside shrine at the scene of the accident at which a candle inside a lantern burned night and day. Mourners visiting the shrine lit their own candles from the main one, pausing for thought and reflection.

Transport Steve's young friends were anxious to convert a sidecar to carry the coffin. Touched by their wish to be involved, Scott and Jenny decided to err on the side of convention, but as a compromise and with their son's love of two wheels in mind, they booked a 'motorcycle hearse' with a 'Clergy Biker' who would also conduct the service. It would be the first time this unique vehicle would be used in Scottish history. On the morning of the funeral the lads arranged to congregate at the greasy spoon café, their favourite meeting place where they joined the cortège. Bikers followed for as far as the eye could see, all moving at an extremely reverent pace.

Location

Fortunately the large chapel at the crematorium had been booked; even so, it was filled beyond capacity. Steve's coffin was carried in and placed on the catafalque by six of his friends dressed in their leathers.

**Service/
Ceremony**

The service, taken by the 'Clergy Biker' began with a CD playing 'Leader of the Pack'.

- The celebration of a life cut short, of Steven Hamish McGill, known to all as Steve, took place.
- A prayer was said.
- A passage was read by a friend from 'When Bad Things Happen to Good People' by Harold Krushner.
- The family had prepared a short biography of Steve's life, which was read out by the 'Clergy Biker'.
- A short silence was observed in Steve's memory.
- At the moment of committal (quite by chance) a mobile phone rang; the quick thinking Reverend put his hand to his ear and said, "Hello, Heaven calling." This eased the sadness of the moment.
- An invitation was extended for everyone to join the family in a nearby hall for heart-warming refreshments.

Refreshments

A number of Jenny's friends had taken responsibility for preparing a welcoming reception. It was early spring and the weather chilly, so steaming bowls of homemade soup were served—Scotch broth and Cullen Skink, Finnan haddock and potato with lots of parsley and hot crusty bread and butter. There were many more mouths to feed than had been anticipated; luckily the soup had started out good and thick! Small tables clothed with white linen and a tartan overlay were placed around the hall, and in the centre of each stood a potted white heather. Chunks of rich butter shortbread were devoured with coffee before everyone took their leave.

Memorial

Steve's friends told Scott and Jenny of their idea to build a memorial cairn of stones in the place they had been going to visit on the day of the accident—high on the moors, a vantage point. The couple were moved by the suggestion and agreed to have a plaque made bearing Steve's name, dates and a special message.

Memorial Ceremony

A lone piper led the procession across the hillside to the place where a stone cairn had been partially built. Steve's ashes were placed inside the cairn, before the final stones were put in place and the plaque added. The assembled family and special friends said their own private farewells before leaving; this place would be visited often for quiet reflection. The piper continued to play Steve's soul on its journey, the haunting sound echoing around the hills.

Reflections

There were many regrets surrounding the loss of this young and unfulfilled life. Although the family grieved deeply, their experience reminded them that Steve had also lived with style and enthusiasm. This memory helped the act of mourning to become a process of healing rather than pain.

Notes:

- Organ donation information. Tel: 0845 6060400. Only 16% of the UK's population are on the NHS Organ Donors Register.
- Motorcycle Funerals: through a funeral director or direct. Tel: 015 3083 4616 (Photograph by Ken Knowles).

LAST ROSE OF SUMMER

A service of remembrance and a churchyard burial followed by an elegant candlelight reception with music to suit the mood. A fund-raising memorial concert took place at a later date.

Introduction

Helen had been widowed for many years and knew that when she died her body would be buried beside her husband in the local churchyard. Her son Stephen, his wife Laura and their two small daughters had a close and loving relationship with Helen. When the time came they planned her funeral to be as individual as she had been. A member of the music circle and the flower club, she had lived her life as a trendy, fashion conscious leader.

Arrangements

When writing her will Helen left instructions for her burial. Rather than take out an insurance or pre-paid funeral plan she invested the money herself in easily available bonds which her family could draw without problems when she died.

Stephen placed all the arrangements in the hands of the Funeral Director who also posted notices of Helen's death with details of the forthcoming funeral service into the appropriate newspapers.

Coffin

Being an architect, Stephen had an eye for design. He was immediately attracted to the stylish lines of the 'Ecopod' coffin. The Ecopod, made from recycled paper, is very strong and light. Although there were several colours and designs to choose from, Stephen chose the pod overlaid with gold leaf, visually stunning and lined with cream coloured feathers. Stephen felt the 'pod' was a fitting vehicle in which Helen would make her final exit. Helen's small granddaughters called it 'Granny's Angel Wagon'.

While Helen's embalmed body lay in the chapel of rest, family and friends visited her in the open coffin. The little girls were anxious to go along too; they wanted to brush Granny's hair, which they had done on many previous occasions. Before the 'Ecopod' was finally closed, they sprinkled her with red rose petals which matched her dress.

Flowers

Four dozen red roses were tied with flowing red and gold ribbons and placed on the gold coffin; the effect was deemed by all as a 'stylish way to go'.

Location

The service of thanksgiving for Helen's life took place in the village church that she had attended for many years. Her friends from the local flower club had arranged dozens of exquisite white lilies, which provided mourners with a fragrant greeting.

<table>
<tr><td>Service/
Ceremony</td><td>

- The children, who wished to attend the service, handed out the 'order of service sheets', on the cover of which was a photograph of Helen and her husband on their wedding day; also, words written in her childhood autograph book by her father: 'Gather ye rosebuds while ye may, old time is a flying. The same sweet rose that blooms today, tomorrow will be dying.'
- Fauré's Requiem played as the coffin was carried into church.
- The Christian service was interspersed with Helen's favourite music.
- Finally, the Vicar thanked those present for their support and on behalf of the family, invited everyone for light refreshments at Stephen and Laura's house nearby, adding that the immediate family would join them following the committal.

At the end of the service, as the coffin was taken into the churchyard, Helen's granddaughters' traced the pathway with red rose petals; the small party led by the Vicar followed the trail to the graveside. Helen was committed to the earth to lie beside her husband. Before leaving they lit a small lantern from which the light would glow well into the evening.
</td></tr>
<tr><td>Refreshments</td><td>It was a late autumn afternoon as everyone gathered in the welcoming warmth of Stephen and Laura's home. Candles flickered from every corner, complementing the dimmed lighting in the large, minimally furnished room. Background music was being played on a grand piano—romantic pieces of a bygone age as caterers served champagne and cups of tea. The family and the Vicar joined the party as trays of dainty savouries and a sumptuous selection of bite-sized cakes were served. On a table in the hall an arrangement of red roses</td></tr>
</table>

stood beside a photograph of Helen and her husband, taken on their last anniversary celebration.

Memorial

Months before her death an evening programme entitled 'A Musical Autobiography' had been presented by a member of the music circle. This idea had inspired Helen to collate her own musical memories with complementary CD's. Sadly, Helen died before it was quite complete, and a friend undertook to bring it up to the very moment. Helen's 'Autobiography in Music' was arranged as a memorial to her and the proceeds from ticket sales were shared between the church roof fund and the National Society for the Prevention of Cruelty to Children for which she had been an active fund raiser.

Helen's name and dates were later added to the existing headstone.

Reflections

Helen's family and friends had let go with love. The occasion had been an uplifting and heart-warming experience for everyone involved, and the children accepted their Grandmother's death quite naturally and spoke of her often.

Notes:

- ARKA Ecopod. Tel: 01273 746011.
  Email: hazel@ecopod.co.uk;
  www.ecopod.co.uk.

- NSPCC: Tel: 01293 449210.

THE WAY WE WERE

A non-religious funeral service for an elderly gentleman of the 'old school' conducted by his granddaughter in a garden of remembrance. After the service everyone celebrated Duncan's life at a champagne reception and lunch at a local hotel. The Funeral Directors took away his body to be cremated.

Introduction   Duncan, a professional gentleman with dignity and polite old-fashioned ways, had been a widower for many years. He had no religious beliefs. His granddaughter Annabel took responsibility for carrying out his wishes that they had discussed together previously.

Arrangements   Annabel, with the help of the Funeral Director, organised and conducted her grandfather's funeral. The service of farewell included contributions by family members and friends.

Rather than settle for a pre-paid funeral scheme, Duncan had put the money into a recoverable investment in Annabel's name, allowing her freedom and flexibility while arranging the funeral. Annabel telephoned friends and relations, giving details of the funeral arrangements and the lunch that was to follow.

Coffin

A solid hardwood casket of traditional design was chosen for Duncan which suited his solid, traditional character.

Flowers

A simple spray of white lilies and rosebuds from the family decorated his coffin. Donations instead of flowers were sent to the Royal National Institute for the Blind (RNIB) which had supported Duncan in his latter years.

Location

The service took place in the unique garden of remembrance that adjoined the Funeral Director's chapel of rest. Having rained earlier in the morning the sun came out and the raindrops sparkled as rows of chairs were placed on the lawn, providing comfortable seating in a peaceful setting.

Service/ Ceremony

Duncan's coffin was waiting in the garden as everyone gathered. Service sheets explained the proceedings which were as follows:

- A cello solo was played by a niece.
- Duncan's granddaughter gave an account of his varied and interesting life.
- An excerpt from an opera, sung unaccompanied by a friend.
- Duncan's three grandsons spoke about memories of their grandfather as small children.
- A neighbour reminisced amusingly, thereby lightening the proceedings.
- A recording of a favourite piece of music was played for quiet reflection.

<u>Transport</u>	Having said goodbye to Duncan, Annabel announced that taxis were waiting to transport everybody to a local hotel for lunch. The funeral directors took his body to the crematorium.
<u>Refreshments</u>	As corks popped, it felt as if Duncan's spirit was there too. Annabel explained, "It was the type of occasion Grandfather had always enjoyed." Following the champagne reception an elaborate cold buffet was served featuring many local delicacies.
<u>Memorial</u>	Duncan's ashes were scattered at a later date with those of his wife, in the same garden of remembrance where days earlier the service had taken place. This beautiful garden is the location of an annual memorial service organised by the funeral directors, after which tea is served.
<u>Reflections</u>	The arrangements had been executed just as Duncan had wished.
<u>Notes:</u>	• Duncan had his pacemaker removed before cremation to avoid explosion; nor was he allowed to take a bottle of his favourite gin for the same reason.
	• Royal National Institute for the Blind. Tel: 020 7388 1266.
<u>Author's Note</u>	Duncan's was one of the funerals I attended that was refreshingly different. The occasion left me with a feeling of excitement, realising there were wider horizons to be explored.

WHEEL OF NATURE

Yvette's pagan funeral was arranged according to her belief that her soul would survive physical death. A night time procession into woodland was led by a drummer with a trumpet heralding the four winds. Following the burial the mourners sat around a brazier singing songs of peace to guitar accompaniment; before leaving they carried out an ancient ritual.

<u>Introduction</u> Yvette's life-long focus had been on nature and the living world. Her love of animals was unmistakable as her fragile body lay surrounded by cats. The sensation of her fingers luxuriating in their fur was comforting, something on which she could focus, and the cats looked especially endearing in the flickering candlelight. Before sliding into unconsciousness Yvette promised her partner Tim that she would return to him, giving him proof of life after death. Recognising that the end was near, Tim gave Yvette permission to "Let go, gently, gently, do not be afraid"—he spoke these words as he opened the window, releasing her soul heavenwards.

Following the Doctor's visit confirming Yvette's death, a nursing friend washed Yvette's body with scented water and wrapped her in a colourful wrap. Friends arranged flowers and foliage around her, sitting in silent prayer at the bedside, creating a time of total peace, knowing that birth, life and death are all part of the same cycle. Her body lay undisturbed in a cool room for several days, allowing the final departure of her spirit.

Arrangements

Yvette believed in God but felt ill at ease with the dogma surrounding the Church hierarchy. Tim and friends who had helped care for her had discussed and understood her wishes for a pagan funeral. She had been pleased with the idea that they would carry out the arrangements themselves, following the guidelines laid out in *The Natural Death Handbook*. Yvette chose to be buried in a woodland glade where she and her friends had often gathered for solar festivals. Permission was granted by the landowner and the guidelines laid out in Appendix Two were adhered to. To enable the funeral to take place as soon as possible, parking and travel information was e-mailed to those journeying from afar. A list of local bed and breakfast establishments was also included. It was recommended that suitable footwear and clothing for a night-time walk be worn.

Coffin

Tim could not bear the thought of Yvette's body being buried naked, as in pagan custom. He wrapped her tenderly in a favourite purple kaftan, covering her with flowers and foliage before closing the lid of her woven willow coffin.

Flowers

Instead of sprays and wreaths, everyone brought with them a collection of gifts from nature—flowers, fruits, nuts, seed heads, shells and more, which would be used during the ceremony.

Transport

Yvette's coffin was transported to the designated meeting place by estate car, then transferred and fixed securely to an ivy clad stretcher for the woodland walk.

Location

Twilight was falling when everyone gathered. Lanterns glowed as the procession, led by a drummer, moved slowly along the woodland path. Through the stillness of the night the drumming echoed and the moonlight illuminated the path which in the Spring had been a carpet of bluebells. A group of people waited beside a charcoal brazier where lanterns were hung in the trees, creating a warm glow by the grave-side.

Ceremony

Together the gathering performed the ancient rites of song, light and mystery which began by scattering their gifts from nature, clockwise, in a circle, around Yvette's coffin, gathering together as the trumpeter heralded the four winds.

- They communed with the Goddess by acknowledging that the physical body consists of four elements—fire, air, water and earth. When Yvette's spirit left her body at death, by the law of nature the four elements reclaimed her:

  Earth that grounds us;
  Water that calms, soothes and heals us;

Air that invigorates us;
and fire which is pure energy.

- The trumpet sounded to the elements as the earth encompassed Yvette's body, which had after all been only a vehicle of her spirit; she was now at one with nature.

- The meaningful words of Kahlil Gibran were read:

    For what it is to die but to stand naked in the wind and to melt into the sun?
    And what it is to cease breathing but to free the breath from its restless tides,
    That it may rise and expand and seek God unencumbered?

- In turn they drank mead from a large crystal chalice and shared bread.

- Everyone joined and sang 'All You Need Is Love' accompanied by the guitar of Yvette's musical friend Teresa who continued to play and sing throughout the evening.

- Many hands made light work as the friends took turns to fill the grave.

- Before leaving, an ancient ritual was performed. The space had been carefully chosen near a yew tree. Yew being the symbol of eternal life, death and re-birth, everyone picked a sprig from the tree, taking turns to burn it on the brazier, their last thoughts rising with the smoke.

Next morning a group retraced the path of the night before; the gifts of nature that had been scattered had provided wildlife with a midnight feast.

Memorial

Yvette's friends remembered her often by visiting the grave on every solar festival, sharing special meals and lighting candles. Tim wishes to be buried beside Yvette when his time comes.

Reflection

An old tradition had been revived by carrying out the funeral themselves. It served to remind them of the hospitality of life and their own mortality.

Notes:

- For burial on private land see Appendix Two.
- Mawdesley Willow Coffins. Tel: 01278 424003.
- *The Natural Death Handbook* offers information on DIY funerals. Tel: 0871 288 2098.
- Theresa Matthew's music for peace gatherings. Tel: 01622 817136.
  Email: Theresa.matthew@ntlworld.com.
- A stretcher to support the coffin was hired from the Red Cross.
- Woven willow chrysalis coffin. The Willow Weave Company : Tel: 01953 887 107. Fax: 01935 457 893.
- The Drummer, James Wilde: Tel: 01903 266994.

TRIBUTE TO OTIS

Tom's guide dog, Otis, had acted as his eyes for thirteen faithful years. The dog's death led Tom, who is still very much alone, to pre-plan his own funeral. Their ashes will eventually be mingled and scattered in the wind from a cliff top.

Introduction

Tom was serving in the Merchant Navy when he lost his sight nineteen years ago. He re-trained in office skills at Loughborough College and with Otis, his first guide dog, set about the challenge of life without sight. Amongst their many remarkable achievements was a ninety-four mile walk along the West Highland Way in Scotland, which they completed in seven days. Otis trained with Tom for the London Marathon, which his master ran on several occasions. Tom now trains, supports and organises leisure activities and holidays for adults and children with sight loss on behalf of the Hampshire Association for the Care of the Blind (HACB).

Arrangements

Taking personal responsibility for his death as he has for his life, Tom made his will, pre-paying his funeral expenses; he also wrote a letter making his wishes known, lodging copies with his solicitor and executor. The extremely close relationship he has with his animals, especially Otis, are a very important part of his plan.

Pet's Remains

Tom's pet rabbit, Harvey, died and was cremated; then followed the death of Otis. Tom hadn't realised he could hurt so much. "I guess it's the price we pay for love!" he said. The ashes of both pets are kept in carved boxes and will be mixed with Tom's remains when the time comes—so they will eventually be together again.

Service

Tom has planned a service at the crematorium, which will include music and memories. The theme tune from the film Pearl Harbour, 'There You'll Be', will be played, and most important of all, 'The Unchained Melody.' "Whenever I hear that song I think of Otis—my eyes fill with tears, that music will haunt me always," Tom reminisced.

Disposal of Remains

Tom's request is that his ashes are mingled with those of his beloved pets and scattered in the wind off the Dorset coast, a place full of peace and tranquillity where Tom had often swum with Otis always by his side and which holds many happy memories.

Tom added with a grin: "I hope whoever scatters the ashes notes which way the wind is blowing."

The poem by W. E. Henley would be very appropriate to be read aloud while scattering the ashes.

The full sea rolls and thunders
In glory and in glee,
O, bury me not in the senseless earth
But in the rolling sea!
Ay, bury me where it surges
A thousand miles from shore,
And in its brotherly unrest
I'll range for evermore.

<u>Quotes</u>

- Tom—"Otis was not only my guide and companion, he was part of me—we were one."
- Tom's sister—"I always knew Tom was safe when I knew he was out with Otis. Otis was full of fun and Tom enjoyed this immensely."
- A Colleague—"You always knew where Tom was in the building when you saw Otis as they were never far apart—he was like his shadow."
- A Friend—"Otis did not mind if he was going out to work or play; all he cared about was being with Tom."
- A Friend—"Otis always greeted people with a smile and this helped Tom with his loss of eye contact."

Note:

- Tom wishes to avoid a gravestone, which has to be tended by others.

Author's Note

Having given confidence and help to so many people, young and old with visual and physical impairment, the example of Tom's courage will live on, leaving the most solid memorial imaginable.

OUT WITH A BANG

A horse-drawn hearse took Sir Richard in style to his funeral. At a lavish party to celebrate his life, a giant rocket containing his ashes exploded into the night sky, becoming one with the universe.

Introduction

Claudia had always been extremely close to her father, especially since her parents' divorce; taking on the role of her mother she proceeded to make the funeral arrangements.

Before her father's death Claudia and he were planning a large party to celebrate their joint birthdays. Claudia decided that the party must continue, becoming a celebration of her father's life.

Arrangements

Sir Richard had made financial provision for his funeral in his will; also enclosed was a letter of his final wishes, that a service take place in the local church followed by cremation. Having put the arrangements into the hands of Funeral Directors, Claudia added her own special touches—ways in which she could express her love for him and acknowledge his adoration of the countryside, farming and horses.

The Funeral Directors confirmed their willingness to accept a coffin made by a carpenter providing it complied with crematoria regulations; they also organised the obituary notices and announcements.

Coffin

Sir Richard's coffin was made with the skill and respect of a craftsman, using the carefully prepared and seasoned wood from an elm blown down in the great storm. It was duly delivered to the Funeral Directors where a nameplate was added bearing Sir Richard's details. His hygienically treated body lay in the chapel of rest where Claudia and other relations visited and were invited to light candles, remaining in the peaceful privacy for as long as they wished.

Flowers

On the morning of the funeral Claudia walked in the fields, alone with her thoughts. She collected armfuls of marguerites, which she arranged in the house, and a large spray of wild flowers, which were to be placed on her father's coffin.

Transport

Two shining black stallions with 'velvets' and dyed black ostrich feathers adorning their heads approached the driveway. Moving at a sedate pace, they drew the glass hearse containing Sir Richard's coffin to a halt at the front door where Claudia put in place the wild flowers she had collected. With her close friends she followed the hearse on foot making their way towards the village church and the tolling bell. The journey took them along country lanes past the fields and animals so familiar to her.

Location

The church had been decorated by the parish flower arrangers; garden flowers festooned every nook and cranny. The bell tolled once for every year of Sir Richard's life. Meanwhile, the congregation waited in the churchyard for the hearse to arrive. The sound of hooves drew nearer and the graceful horses eventually halted at the lych gate. The Vicar led the coffin borne by six of Sir Richard's employees into the church, where everyone took their place.

Service/ Ceremony

A celebration of the life of Sir Richard, known to many as 'Dickie', was tempered with sadness and thankfulness following his sudden illness. The service proceeded as follows:

- Introductory prayers, hymns and readings.
- The address, given by Claudia, covered her father's life from birth to that moment. She mentioned his heart being of pure gold, being at his happiest buying and selling horses—horse racing had been his favourite pastime. She spoke of the three 'F's' being most important to him: family, friends and farm, and if anybody was under 60 years old they were automatically 'boy' or 'girl'. She asked the congregation to remember him in their own way, adding that he believed in making every day a Christmas Day.
- Prayers and hymns followed.
- A school friend spoke of their joint escapades as lads, and also mentioned that the first and last time he had seen 'Dickie' had been with horses.
- After the final prayer the Vicar explained that the committal would take place at the church gate.
- On behalf of Claudia he thanked everyone for their support and issued invitations for light

refreshment, which would be served at the family home.

Music was played as the procession made its way to the church gate where the committal took place.

The Fesian Blacks, with their patient temperament, waited as mourners crowded to say goodbye to Sir Richard. The coffin would be taken to the place where the horse transport was parked, then transferred to a motor hearse for the journey to the crematorium. The Vicar would accompany the deceased; it had been his wish to go this way.

Refreshment

Drinks and light refreshments were served as mourners wandered in the garden, exchanging memories or just sitting in shady places remembering.

Celebration Party

At a later date Claudia sent out invitations decorated with a cosmic theme, inviting guests to a party to be held on her father's birthday to celebrate his life. Via a red carpet, guests made their way into the marquee to be greeted by Claudia where a harpist played and drinks and canapés were being served. The marquee draped in navy and white had a night sky from which a million tiny stars twinkled down on the formally laid tables. Navy linen scattered with stars and moons reflected the theme and an abundance of white flowers and candles decorated every table. Each place was named. Beside Claudia a spare place setting had been laid for her father, in which a special candle burned.

The menu covers were decorated with a photograph of Sir Richard and the words from Shakespeare's *Romeo and Juliet*:

"Take him and cut him out in little stars and he will make the face of heaven so fine that all the world will be in love with the night."

The meal was announced by a Master of Ceremonies, which we served from a well-equipped service tent. After dinner speeches and entertainment were announced by the MC:

- Two arranged speeches
- Readings and music
- A tribute from a retired employee
- Anecdotes from friends and compatriots
- Claudia thanked everyone for coming.

As midnight approached everyone was asked to move outside where champagne was served. A dazzling firework display ended with a trumpet fanfare followed by a 'big bang', as the rocket containing some of Dickie's ashes rose 70m before exploding in a shower of stars into the night sky. A champagne toast was drunk to a dear father, relative, and friend.

Memorial

As her own personal memorial to her father, Claudia commissioned a 'diamond' to be made from the remaining ashes, which she would have crafted into a ring. She felt comfort in the fact that he would always be with her. Claudia posted the ashes to be converted into a 'diamond' with a copy of the cremation certificate firmly attached.

Claudia had a dozen Scots' Pines planted on the estate, hoping that one day red squirrels would be attracted to them.

A stained glass window for the local church was designed, made and dedicated in Sir Richard's memory.

Reflections

The day of the funeral had been one of happy memories for Claudia, and she was pleased to have had the courage to give the address herself. The celebration party had been an occasion of joy and a profoundly healing experience.

Notes:

- A horse-drawn hearse may be hired either through a reputable funeral director or direct. Tel: Cribbs 020 7746 1855.
- Sir Richard's bequest left to charity was not liable for inheritance tax.
- The deceased also owned property abroad for which he made a separate will.
- Fireworks—as far as the author is aware no company advertises this service, but the idea was discussed with several manufacturers and not dismissed.
- Cremated ashes made into 'Diamonds': www.lifegems.com

GOING WILD

With a desire to return to nature I have chosen to make my own willow coffin ready for a Green woodland burial along with special childhood toys, to be followed by cream teas and a champagne toast to friendship.

<u>Introduction</u> Whilst researching for this book, ideas for my own funeral have changed many times. My love and concern for Mother Earth and the environment are reflected in my choice of a Green and ecologically friendly woodland burial. Knowing that death often comes suddenly with no time to plan, I wanted to be prepared for this inevitable event. My children, being directors of their own media company, constantly work to tight deadlines (excuse the pun!). Making my own arrangements will relieve them of additional burdens. I expect at this moment they dismiss it as another of mother's wacky ideas!

Arrangements

Premium bonds purchased in my son's name will ensure that expenses can easily be covered; being a tax free investment, his personal finances will not be complicated. Both children are aware of my current wishes and know the whereabouts of the relevant documents, including my will, living will and letter of advance funeral wishes.

Coffin

My choice of coffin is based on the ecological requirements for my chosen woodland burial, which includes no embalming.

My daughter recently thrust a page from a magazine at me containing details of a willow-coffin-making workshop. I intend to book a place on the next course and make my own coffin which, until required, will make a perfect container for the piles of paperwork that clutter my study; stuffed tightly, it will double as a window seat for the dog!

When the time comes, I would like to be snuggled in a cosy blanket in the embrace of Mother Earth, surrounded by my collection of soft toys, especially threadbare moth-eaten Mr Ted, Monkey and Panda, which were presents to me at birth and have always been an integral part of my life. Also to take with me all the special cards collected over the years, many made by my children at infant school.

Flowers

I would like everyone to bring one single flower or item of nature, which has a symbolic link to our friendship.

On a hot street in India, I saw to my horror a young bear putting on a show which I learned lasted up to 12 hours a day. He was being forced up on to his hind legs in a macabre 'dance' to entertain tourists. Any donations are to be made to the World Society for the Protection of Animals (WSPA); this would be so close to my heart and help stop such cruelty.

Transport

I don't mind how I get there, but there will no doubt be some form of horse trailer available within the family to take me to my resting place. The wooden bier at the burial ground will be ideal for wheeling the coffin through the woodland to my grave.

Location

I have visited my chosen burial place on several occasions. The many acres of tranquil woodland set amidst the chalky South Downs with fields of sheep beyond immediately captured my imagination. On a glorious day the dappled sunlight twinkles through the trees, or on a wet day, armed with umbrella and wellies, it is still easy to blend with nature and the seasons. The environment creates the perfect natural haven for birds, animals, native plants and trees, ensuring preservation of the woodland.

Service/ Ceremony

Rev. Lesley Edwards, founder of Choice Farewells and a dear friend, has created a short ceremony for my departure. If the weather is good it is to take place at the graveside, otherwise in the pleasant rooms at the Sustainability Centre.

- Lesley will read aloud a letter written by me to my children—based on my departure to the kitchens of (hopefully) heaven.

- The Buddhist Mustard Seed fable is to be read aloud.

- If my friend Lizzy Laird is willing and able, I would like her to sing something light-hearted, reflecting nature and the beautiful surroundings.
- The four elements—the words of the ceremony are to be read out in accordance with the four elements: air, water, fire and earth—turning to face the four points of the compass, the last being earth when we face the grave.
- As my coffin is lowered into its cosy hay-lined nest, it will be covered in the flowers that my family and friends have chosen to bring.
- I want there to be mention of my strong belief in reincarnation and that this life was just one of many past and present.
- My deep, melting love for animals would be satisfied if a small, wild creature, one that has been injured and nursed back to health, could be released into the safe haven. If appropriate, I would love my little granddaughter to carry out this task.

Refreshments

At the end of the ceremony Lesley would issue an invitation for everybody to stay for 'crem teas'. ('Crem teas' being a play on words which was often used while catering for funerals!) These will be served in the well-equipped Sustainability Centre with a champagne toast to love and friendship. My catering friends always jested that being so organised I would have the food ready in my freezers—sorry to disappoint them! Before leaving, everyone will be asked to sign a special book made of handmade paper also containing the words of the service to be given to my children.

Memorial

A tree to mark my grave would be perfect, a species covered in winter berries to feed the birds. Within a short while wild flowers of the habitat will grow naturally back to cover the chalky earth.

Reflections

Having planned my funeral and looked death in the face, I am aware of a feeling of relief and am now free to get on and live my life fully.

Notes:

- The ceremony has been planned by Rev. Lesley Edwards, founder of Choice Farewells. Tel: 023 8086 1256: www.choiceceremonies.co.uk
- Windrush Willow Coffin weaving workshops. Tel: 01395 233669; www.windrushwillow.com
- WSPA (World Society for the Protection of Animals). Tel: 020 7793 0208; www.wspa.org.uk
- Living Will Forms and Forms of Advance Funeral Wishes can be obtained from the Natural Death Centre. Tel: 0871 288 2098.
- ARKA are a funeral/life celebrat company in Brighton with whom I have close connections. (Also manufacturer of the ecopod.) I would like my colleagues at ARKA to support my family when the time comes to carry out my funeral. Their knowledge of woodland burial is unsurpassable, as is their sensitivity and attention to detail. ARKA Original Funerals: Tel: 01273 766620
- Ancient burials took place in a special place where family and friends—'the tribe'—could be together. Since writing this book, many of my friends like the idea of being buried in the same woodland setting—together again!
- It is important to me to stress to my children that in spite of my having written down my funeral wishes, when the time comes they must do what feels right for them.

FINAL THOUGHT
By the Rev. Lesley Edwards BTH MA MIFC

The farewell ceremonies in this book are not gimmicky 'send offs'—nor are they making light of death. Far from it, they come from a deep desire to acknowledge the unique essence of every human being. Each ceremony recognises that every life is of special value and that when we finally die we will all have something exceptional to leave behind—a legacy far more than mere possessions. We may leave a store of achievements or just a wacky sense of humour, but more often it is just simply our unquantifiable selves that someone somewhere will always cherish in their hearts. It is what the ceremonies in this book do best—celebrate individual lives.

So often the standard form of words at a crematorium or chapel seem to drone over our heads and we come away from a funeral feeling more forlorn, more bereft than ever. Somehow added to our grief is an underlying depression stemming from a feeling of hopelessness. We feel that this beloved person has at the end barely been noticed. At the door as we leave are the next mourners, queuing to get this morbid business over and done with.

Ideally our final ceremony in this life should be an uplifting and inspiring occasion and a celebration—a celebration that brings hope and comfort to family and friends, leaving memories untarnished by sadness.

APPENDIX ONE
CHECK LIST

LOCATE APPROPRIATE DOCUMENTS		SERVICE SHEETS	
THEME		REFRESHMENTS	
DATE		MEMORIAL	
TIME		ANNIVERSARY CELEBRATION	
LOCATION OF SERVICE/CEREMONY			
LOCATION OF CREMATION/BURIAL			
NEWSPAPER NOTICES			
COFFIN			
FLOWERS			
TRANSPORT			
CONTENTS OF SERVICE			

APPENDIX TWO
BURIAL ON PRIVATE LAND

The author recommends that anybody considering burial on private land should contact The Natural Death Centre, to check practicalities, guidelines and current burial laws before commencing arrangements. The Natural Death Centre, London Tel: 0871 288 2098; www.naturaldeath.org.uk.

Note to readers in the USA and Canada

Burial laws differ from state to state. For general information and the location of woodland burial sites, contact The Natural Death Centre, London Tel: +44(0)871 288 2098; www.naturaldeath.org.uk.

APPENDIX THREE
SOME USEFUL ADDRESSES

- ARKA Original Funerals, 39-41 Surrey Street, Brighton, BN1 3PB. Tel: 01273 766620

- British Buddhist Association
  11 Biddulph Road, London, W9 1JA Tel:-020 7286 5575

- Choice Farewells.
  107 Salisbury Road, Totton, Southampton, SO40 3HZ Tel: 023 8086 1256 Website:—www.choiceceremonies.co.uk
  Email: Lesley@choiceceremonies.co.uk

- Civil Funerals
  PO Box 160, St. Neots, Cambridgeshire. PE19 5WL Tel:-01480 810500
  Website: www.civilceremonies.co.uk

- Lesbian and Gay Christian Movement.
  Oxford House, Derbyshire Street, London. E2 6HG Tel: 020 7739 1249

- Independent Funerals Advisory Services (IFAS)
  PO Box 1, Watched, Somerset. TAZ3 OAG Tel:-01984 632285

- National Association of Bereavement Services
  20 Norton Folgate, London E1 6DB
  24 hour telephone helpline Tel: 020 7247 1080

- National Association of Funeral Directors
  618 Warwick Road, Solihull, West Midlands, B91 1AA. Tel: 0121 711 1343

- Registrar General
  General Register Office, Smedley Hydro, Trafalgar Road, Berkdale, Southport, PR8 2HH. Tel: 0151 471 4200

- British Humanist Association
  1 Gower Street, London, WC1E 6HD
  Tel: 020 7430 0908
  Email: info@humanism.org.uk
  www.humanism.org.uk

- The Association of Interfaith Ministers & Spiritual Counsellors
  Halsecombe House, Parsons Hill, Porlock, Somerset, TA24 8QP.
  Tel: 01643 862621. Website:—www.interfaithministers.org.uk
  Email: halsecombe@aol.com

- The Natural Death Centre
  6 Blackstock Mews Blackstock Road London, N4 2BT
  www.naturaldeath.org.uk
  Email: ndc@alberyfoundation.org.uk

- The Unitarian & Free Christian Churches
  Central Administration Office, Essex Hall, Essex Street, London, WC2R 3HY.
  Tel: 020 7240 2384

- United Reformed Church
  86 Tavistock Place, London, WC1H 9RT. Tel: 020 7916 2020

For local information on places to worship and religious organisations,
see Yellow Pages.

APPENDIX FOUR
RECOMMENDED READING

- *Alternative Funerals*
  by Kate Gordon, published by Constable

- *Ceremonies for Life*
  by Michael Jordan, published by Collins & Brown

- *Dead Happy*
  by Lance Trendall, published by LTP

- *Funerals without God*
  British Humanist Association

- *Illuminata: Thoughts, Prayers, Rites of Passage*
  by Marianne Williamson, published by Random House

- *Life After Life*
  by Raymond A Moody JR, MD, published by Bantam Books

- *Life Lessons*
  by Elizabeth Kübler-Ross and David Kessler, published by Simon and Schuster

- *Many Lives, Many Masters*
  Through Time into Healing
  by Dr Brian Weiss, published by Piatkus

- *One Step at a Time* (mourning a child)
  by Betty Mandell, published by Floris Books

- *Past Lives and Present Dreams*
  by Denise Linn, published by Piatkus

- *The American Way of Death*
  by Jessica Mitford, published by Virgo

- *The Dead Good Funeral Book*
  by Sue Gill and John Fox.

- *The New Age Handbook on Death and Dying*
  by Carol E Parrish-Harra PhD, published by Sparrow Hawk Piers

- *The Natural Death Handbook*
  Published by Rider (2003)

- *The Tibetan Book of Living and Dying*
  Published by Random House

- *Unblock Your Emotions: Lazy Person's Guide to Emotional Healing*
  by Doctor Andrew Trissidder. Published by New Leaf.

- *Who Dies?*
  by Stephen Lavine, published by Cygnus Books.

My epitaph

ABOUT THE AUTHOR

Until recently Jean Francis owned her own catering company, co-ordinating the many different occasions that mark life's milestones such as birth, marriage and death. Jean was inspired to write this *When It's Time to Go* following some very moving funerals she herself attended. She realises that these occasions do not have to be merely an event to "go through" but can provide a real opportunity to give a very personal tribute to the deceased and what their lives stood for.

When It's Time to Go is published in association with Diadem Books
www.diadembooks.com/funerals.htm

0-595-31859-2

Printed in the United States
43897LVS00005B/88